THE
BAREFOOT
INDIAN

THE MAKING OF
A MESSIAHRESS

JULIA HEYWOOD

BOOKS

Winchester, U.K.
New York, U.S.A.

First published by O Books, 2007
O Books is an imprint of John Hunt Publishing Ltd.,
The Bothy, Deershot Lodge, Park Lane, Ropley, Hants, SO24 0BE, UK
office1@o-books.net
www.o-books.net

Distribution in:

UK and Europe
Orca Book Services
orders@orcabookservices.co.uk
Tel: 01202 665432
Fax: 01202 666219 Int. code (44)

USA and Canada
NBN
custserv@nbnbooks.com
Tel: 1 800 462 6420
Fax: 1 800 338 4550

Australia and New Zealand
Brumby Books
sales@brumbybooks.com.au
Tel: 61 3 9761 5535
Fax: 61 3 9761 7095

Far East (offices in Singapore,
Thailand, Hong Kong, Taiwan)
Pansing Distribution Pte Ltd
kemal@pansing.com
Tel: 65 6319 9939
Fax: 65 6462 5761

South Africa
Alternative Books
altbook@peterhyde.co.za
Tel: 021 447 5300
Fax: 021 447 1430

Text copyright Julia Heywood 2007

Design: Jim Weaver

ISBN-13: 978 1 84694 040 8
ISBN-10: 1 84694 040 0

A CIP catalogue record for this book is available from the
British Library.

Printed in the US by Maple Vail

CONTENTS

Have you ever had an event
in your life when you know life
will never be the same again…?

1

THE FIRM

It was when I responded to the following ad that I knew my life would change forever!

Blimey! I was never given this option at school by the careers adviser, I thought. I was bemused by such an ad but intrigued. Surely it must be some kind of spoof. My curiosity got the better of me so I sent in my details and by return I received the following application form. I filled this in to the best of my ability and with total honesty, but in my opinion I did not come across as impressive, in fact I seemed the least likely person they would be looking for.

Application form for the position of Messiah/Messiahress

Please answer all questions with total honesty!

Age: *42*
Gender: *Female*
Qualifications: *None*
Achievements to date: *None*
Do you think life could be better? *Absolutely!*
Do you know the meaning of life? *Haven't got a clue*
Do you believe in God? **Yes!*
As a whole, what is your view of mankind? *Lost*
If someone came to you for help, what would you do? *Run away*
If you could do anything in the world, what would it be? *Leave it*
Do you judge people? *All the time*
Do you know who & what makes all life possible? *No, I've never thought about it*
Are you serene, calm & still? *Never*
Can you heal the sick? *I've never tried*
Can you walk on water? *Probably not*
If 5,000 people needed feeding what would you do? *Contact McDonalds*
Do you love your neighbor? *Yes – when they turn the hi-fi down*
Please say why you would like this job....
I could say that I am a considerate and compassionate person who cares about others and the state of the world. I'd be lying. The reality is I need cash! Money doesn't grow on trees but then in your organization it probably does!!

Thank you. Please email this form back to JC@I-am.org.uk

*I thought I'd better answer this with 'yes' considering the job description.

So there it was, the completed application form. When I nervously pressed the send button I still wasn't sure that this was for real but at least they weren't asking for any money. Having sent it off, I pushed it to the back of my mind and started on the pile of ironing.

Two weeks passed and I still hadn't had a reply but I presumed that they must have been inundated with applications. Either that or I was now part of a TV program scheduled to be shown on April Fool's day!

Finally the wait was over, three weeks later I received a reply via email.

> Dear Applicant,
>
> Thank you for your recent application for the position of Messiahress.
>
> We are pleased to inform you that we would very much like to meet with you regarding the above position.
>
> Having gone through your application form we feel that you are a potential candidate and have put you on our short list.
>
> We would like to interview you on Sunday 8 March at 12.00 noon, please confirm that this is convenient. We will then send you the address and directions of where the interview will take place.
>
> Yours sincerely
> JC
> Managing Director
>
> P.S. the only thing you need to bring is yourself.

March 8, was my birthday and Sunday was an unusual day to hold an interview; I thought that was a day of rest. Anyway, I confirmed that the date was OK and received the directions and location. So off I went. I was still uncertain of what I was letting myself in for but curiosity was definitely getting the better of me.

It was an early start for me as one likes to look one's best when going for an interview. It took me two hours to get ready and four hours to get there. On approaching the building I was amazed at how tall it was, it was the highest tower block I had ever seen. I entered the reception and looked at the floor plan to see which floor the office of I'AM was on; it was on the Top floor in 'The Unlimited Suite'.

There was no way I was taking the stairs, so off I went in the elevator. My stomach was churning and I remember thinking 'what the hell am I doing, I have no idea about the people I am about to meet; they could be psychopaths!' The lift eventually came to a halt; basically it couldn't go any further. The doors opened. 'Here goes' I whispered under my breath as I stepped out of the elevator.

I looked around and found a door which said 'The Unlimited Suite'. I approached it and was just about to knock when the door began to open on its own. I stepped through and couldn't believe what I was seeing.

It was the plushest office I had ever seen and the light was dazzling. Sunlight was flooding through the windows. Comfort just oozed from every corner of the room, which was very large, light and airy with a subtle smell of jasmine. A sense of calm and stillness filled the room and I immediately felt at ease. At the far end, people sat around the largest of tables but they were too far away for me to make out who they were.

"Please come over," said a voice from the far end. "You are most welcome."

As I got nearer the people became clearer and my jaw began to drop, literally, for around the table sat 'prophets', 'miracle workers', 'wise men', 'spiritual teachers', 'enlightened beings', 'gurus', 'sages'; whatever you want to label them the room was full of them! I had never seen such an extraordinary sight.

When I reached the table all my anxiety seemed to melt away. The compassion radiating from these people was unlike anything I had experienced or seen before. In their eyes was a depth that seemed to go on forever and their smiles were as reassuring as the sun rising everyday. I felt at home, for the first time in my life I felt like I belonged.

"Please take a seat," said JC, the Managing Director, who sat at the head of the table. "We are very pleased you have come today." He continued, "I shall briefly explain about this exciting job opportunity that has interested you enough to come here today.

Now, to get to the position of Messiahress involves an extensive training program and it is not an easy path to follow. Once you have decided, here today, to walk this path you will not be able to get off it. Do you understand?"

"Er, yes." I replied gingerly.

"To arrive at the ultimate goal may not be easy. It all depends on the trainee. The training can be very hard, and there may be times when you wish you had never started but all this is part of the process. When you feel ready, you will have to sit an exam, during the training you will also be assessed and marked along the way; on passing the exam you will be awarded the certificate of Messiahress. Your understanding will be complete."

"To help you we have appointed a very special lady who has gone through what you are about to go through, she will be there with you whenever you ask her to be. Her wisdom knows no bounds. We also, here at Head Office, will contact you periodically to encourage you or to point you in the right direction if needed. Just keep in mind the ultimate job, 'the promotion' and the rewards will be beyond anything you can imagine."

Sounds good I thought, although I really didn't understand what he was talking about!

As we sat around chatting the food began to arrive. I have never seen a spread like it and the taste was divine. The food seemed to appear from thin air, I certainly didn't see any caterers in the room but then anything was possible considering the company I was keeping. Then, as if from nowhere, stood the most beautiful woman I had ever seen. She had the most amazing long black hair which shone like silk when the light caught it and her skin was a flawless olive color. I had never seen such beauty; it was hard to take my eyes off her. Her whole appearance was breathtaking.

"Hello," she said as she came over to me "I am The Barefoot Indian. I will be your training coach."

Her voice was very welcoming, yet it had a quality of authority and certainty about it.

"Pleased to meet you" I said whilst quickly glancing down to look at her feet. She did not have any shoes on but was wearing a beautiful ankle bracelet, studded with turquoise stones.

She progressed in a sweet voice "I will be with you whenever you need me, just think of me and I will be there. I will answer any questions you may have but the responsibility to understand the answers is down to you."

"Do you have any questions for me now?"

"Yes," I said "If you don't mind me asking, why are you called The Barefoot Indian? Do you not like wearing shoes?"

She smiled and replied "It is a Red Indian tribal tradition that when a baby is born the parents name the baby after the first thing they see. I was a difficult birth and came out feet first. The first thing my Father saw was my bare feet poking out; hence he called me The Barefoot Indian."

How lovely I thought, I started to ponder what my parents first saw when I was born and was filled with horror at what I could have been named: 'coal in bucket' 'pipe in ashtray' 'wonky picture on wall.' They somehow didn't seem to have the same ring about them.

I brought myself back to the present moment. As quickly as The Barefoot Indian appeared she left. I was sure I would have many questions for her later.

I continued to sit around chatting with all these wonderful people; I hadn't felt this relaxed in ages. They put me at total ease, an ease that I had not felt until today. I got the feeling that it didn't matter what I looked like or what ridiculous things came out of my mouth, they had no judgment of me, in fact I got the sensation that they were seeing something in me that I could not see.

"I have to say that this office is wonderful, if I qualify as Messiahress will I work from here?" I asked.

A little tubby man sitting crossed legged with his eyes shut in the corner of the room in what looked like the most painful yoga position replied "absolutely!"

I continued "Why did you pick such a tall building to work from?"

At this point JC stood up and walked over to the window and beckoned me over.

"This building is perfect; it's all to do with perspective."

Curiously I asked, "What do you mean?"

"Life is about perspective; whatever your perspective is determines what you experience." He went on "Up here we have a very different perspective on the world. We can look down and see what's going on. For example, take a look at that woman over there in the park."

I followed the direction of his pointed finger and could just make out a woman in the park who was clearly distressed.

"She was walking her dog when it got off the lead and ran away. She is very distressed and cannot find her beloved dog. Now, from our perspective up here we can see where the dog is."

I followed his finger again and sure enough there was the dog rummaging in the bushes about half a mile away from the woman.

"To us the dog is not lost, we can see the whole picture. If the woman could see what we see, look at the world from our perspective, would she be distressed?"

"Well no, she would just go to where her dog is." I said.

"Exactly! All she needs to do is change her perspective, see the whole picture and there is no distress, the dog was never lost."

"But how can she change her perspective?" I enquired.

"She just needs to accept that there is another perspective, even if she can't see it immediately but just entertained the thought that there might be one she would see it, it would come to her. All would be revealed."

How obvious I thought. This made me think that maybe this was why none of my prayers were answered. In my moments of desperation, that to which I was praying was not seeing what I was seeing. From its perspective things appeared to be very different.

I stood for a while looking down on the world. I could see people rushing around totally unaware that there was another viewpoint. From where I stood the world looked vast with unlimited potential, from where they stood they couldn't see beyond their own noses. It also struck me that from where I stood I could see where a person had come from and I could see where they were going. If I were to speak of what I saw the world would call me psychic, they would be convinced that I had special powers. I giggled to myself.

I returned to the table and began to eat some fruit which tasted unlike any fruit I had ever had and clearly had not been sitting on a supermarket shelf!

"Can I ask you something?" I asked JC.

"Anything" he replied.

"Why do you need a new trainee? Surely any one of you could go out there and do your stuff. You have far more experience than I could ever have."

"Do not underestimate yourself. But to answer your question, as one of us once said, 'you cannot tread on the same piece of water twice.' Life is full of experience; once an experience is fulfilled you move on to the next. There are infinite experiences. You can only move forward not back."

"But you must have noticed that there are great atrocities in the world which are done in your names, where it is claimed that wars exist because it is your will. Would it not be wise to put the record straight?"

"Only the fearful and weak need to use another's name in order to fight a battle, they haven't got the guts to stand up and say 'I am doing this because this is what I think.' 'I do this in my name.' 'This is my will.' To do this they would have to be challenged and justify why they think what they think. Instead they use the invisible, that which cannot be challenged. It is an excuse to express what is in their minds and clearly not ours. We have never been consulted. It is not our will."

"But couldn't you stop them from doing such things?"

"Only the one who starts something has the power within them to stop something."

"You put things so simply!" I exclaimed.

"Life is not complicated" he replied.

Time was moving on and I was concerned about making my way home. I stood up and suggested that I make a move. I felt that very little was discussed regarding the job position but somehow this didn't seem to matter.

"We would very much like to offer you the position if you would like it" said JC

"Yes, I think I would, especially if it means working here with you guys! How long does the training last?"

"That is down to you, it all depends on your speed of progress." said Mr Chang, a Chinese chap with the longest plaits I have ever seen.

"And what about the pay?" I enquired.

"All your needs are taken care of," Mr Chang said with a reassuring smile.

JC continued "You must now go back to your life and live it as normal; the training will begin when you wake-up tomorrow."

"Do you have an instruction booklet or training manual that I could use?" I asked.

"All that you need is with you. Do not think about tomorrow, tomorrow will take care of itself. To help you on your way, keep in mind at all times, no matter what is going on around you, that there is only one solution to any problem. There is only one thing to ever know."

"And what is that?" I enquired.

"That is for you to discover," he replied with a grin.

This is all very confusing but intriguing at the same time, I thought.

"Just one more thing," I said nervously, "Will I ever get to meet the Chairman, the head of the Company?"

"Well, let me put it this way, on the day of your promotion, yes, you will most definitely meet the 'Head', the one in charge!" he smiled.

As I was putting on my coat to leave I enquired what the time was, I felt like I had been there such a long time I was certain that my parking ticket would have ran out.

"I'm afraid we do not know the time, but there is a clock in the elevator" said Mr Chang.

"OK, bye then!" I shouted as I left the room.

I pressed for the elevator and waited impatiently. I was in a hurry to get back to the car; I could not afford a parking fine. At last it arrived, I stepped in, pressed the button and looked at the clock and it said twelve noon. It must be wrong, I thought. The elevator stopped and I stepped out.

"What time is it please?" I asked a gentleman who was waiting to get in the elevator.

"Twelve noon" he replied.

REFLECTIONS

I awoke the next day refreshed and leapt out of bed, well not quite, but my vigor was great compared to most mornings. As I ate breakfast I contemplated what I should do for the day.

'Live life as normal' JC's words came back to me.

OK, I thought, I shall just take it easy today, watch a bit of TV and see what happens, if anything. After all this was the first day of my new job and there didn't seem to be any rules.

After spending the day chilling out and enjoying my new job, by mid afternoon I began to ponder The Barefoot Indian. I couldn't get her striking beauty out of my mind. No sooner had I started to think of her than there was a knock at the door. I opened the door and there she stood. In my amazement, I invited her in.

"What would you like to ask me?" she enquired.

"Well, erm," I stumbled "I am so struck by your beauty, your skin is flawless, your figure is to die for and there is not a hair out of place. Your beauty is so natural, you wear no make up and yet your features are highlighted by some kind of invisible source. How do you achieve that? I can spend two hours getting ready, slapping on lotions and potions, applying make up that needs a chisel to remove it and yet when I look in the mirror, my efforts don't come anywhere near the level of your beauty."

"Perhaps that's where your error lies," she answered.

"Where?" I asked.

"With the mirror," she said and then continued "I don't need a mirror to show me what I look like. I have seen what I am without a mirror."

Intrigued, I asked "What do you mean?"

"Let me put it this way. Imagine looking into a pond and seeing the reflection of a flower. Firstly, your ability to see the reflection is dependant on many influences, for example the movement of the water, the light, and the weather to name a few. One day the clarity of the water may be murky so the reflection appears dull, you would prefer it if it was clear. The next day the water may be moving so the reflection looks distorted, you would prefer it to be calm. The next day the lighting is bad so the reflection is dark, you would prefer it to be bright. You are never happy with your view of the reflection, it's never perfect."

I agreed.

She continued "let's assume that finally the day comes when all the conditions are right, you are able to see the reflection of the flower in all its glory. The reflection is perfect."

"Can you smell and experience the sweet fragrance of the flower from the reflection?"

"No," I said.

"Are you able to touch and experience the delicate structure of its petals from the reflection?"

"No."

"Can you hold the flower in your hands, marvel at its beauty and experience its innocence from the reflection?"

"No."

"Why not?"

"Well, because it's a reflection, an image only. It is not the flower. It has no life on its own."

"Correct. The only way to truly behold the flower is to go to the source of the reflection! You have become so obsessed with the reflection that you have forgotten the source. There and only there can you experience the beauty of the flower and all that it is. The flower is a living thing for you to embrace. Go to the source!"

"You are concerned with your own reflection; this will not

reveal your true beauty, only the source can do that."

"Finally, when you have gone to the source and seen what is there, would you then need to check the reflection?" she asked.

"Well no, concern with the reflection was because the source of it had not been seen," I replied.

"That's right and so it is with you. Go to the source of you, not the reflection; it is the only way to experience your true beauty!"

"But how do you go to the source?" I asked.

"Stop being concerned with the reflection. See it for what it is; a reflection. When you turn away from the reflection only the source remains."

She continued, "Practice this little exercise. On a piece of paper write down everything you know about your appearance and everything you know about yourself. Describe yourself in detail, but do not write down anything that you have seen in a reflection or have been told by someone else. By doing this, it will give you some idea of how well you know yourself. Do this periodically and see how it changes."

As she spoke, in my mind, I briefly tried to do what she was saying.

"It seems impossible," I said.

"Persevere with it. You will have to draw on knowledge that is in you that has been kept hidden for so long, and you will have to use senses and feelings that you have long forgotten how to use. No matter how obscure things may feel, write them down."

"I will" I promised.

She then left.

I grabbed a notebook and a pen, headed the page ME, and eagerly set about the task only to find the paper remained blank. I guess that's the end of mirrors for me! I thought.

3

THE SUBLIME AND THE RIDICULOUS

I still wasn't clear about my new job and what was expected of me. It appeared that I had no direction and was being left to my own devices. As this was the case and I had not been given anything specific to do I decided to visit a dear friend of mine. He was approaching eighty and was quite infirm and loved company. His wife had died about seven years ago and he missed her terribly, to the point where you would think that he had just lost her. I loved to visit him as I found him so interesting and he always had a story to tell.

I set off and on the way there I started to think of how I could help him. Perhaps I could heal him? My mind started to wander. How would I heal him? Maybe all I need to do is say get up and walk! That's been done before; it's worked for the others, why not for me? Maybe with my new job position I had been given special powers. Then horror struck me as I imagined the headlines: 'it's a miracle, man gets up and walks, then falls down the stairs!'

I shall leave the healing for now, I thought, I need further advice on that one!

I arrived at my friend's house and walked in to the room where he was sitting.

"Hello," he said, "how wonderful to see you. You look so well, what have you been doing to yourself? You look different!"

"Do I?" I replied. "I'm not sure."

I really couldn't answer him as I had not looked in a mirror for what seemed like a long time.

We sat chatting, drinking tea and eating cake. It was very pleasant. After a while he began talking to a photograph of his wife which sat on the table next to him. It was positioned directly in his vision so he could always see it. He always spoke to her as if she was in the room and kept her informed of what he was up to. The photo was the last one that was ever taken of her; she was in her wheelchair and struggling to smile for the camera. How sad for him, I thought.

I began to bring him up to date on the gossip from the local village; he loved to hear all the news. I had been talking for about five minutes, when I suddenly noticed he had dropped off to sleep. All the drugs he took had this effect, so he would say; either that or I just bored him! So I sat quietly whilst he had a little nap.

After about five minutes I suddenly had the sensation that we were not alone but I knew no one had come into the room. The feeling grew stronger but I did not feel alarmed. Then, out of the corner of my eye I glimpsed something. My head turned and there standing in the corner of the room was a woman. I jumped slightly but her presence made me feel at ease. It was the same ease I felt the day I went to Head Office.

She stood smiling at me. As I looked at her it became apparent to me that it was his wife. I had never met her but I could tell from the photograph that it was her, the eyes were the same. Her body was in perfect health. She had an ageless quality about her and the same essence of beauty radiated from her just like The Barefoot Indian although her appearance was unique.

"Don't feel sad for him," she said "I am here."

"He can't see where I am because he is always looking at where I am not."

"What do you mean?" I asked.

"He looks at that photograph and sees me there. All his thoughts are on memories of what was. His attention is on something that isn't living. Everywhere he looks he reminds himself of where I used to be, he never once thinks about where I am. How could he possibly see me when he has frozen me in a place where I am not?"

"Well, he can't," I replied "But how does he see where you are?"

"By ceasing to look where I am not!"

"Let me ask you, if you were to leave the room now and he woke up and wanted to talk to you, what would he do, how would he do it?" she asked.

"Well, he would have to find me, contact me, seek me out." I replied.

"That's right, he would make the effort to find you and he would go to where you are. Why should I be different?" she went on. "Death is a trick, an illusion. I haven't gone anywhere; I am very much alive, here and now. To him I left the world, to me the world left me."

"Why am I able to see you?" I asked.

"You have willingness and nothing more" She replied.

"I am so glad I have seen you. It's a pleasure to meet you." I said.

"The pleasure is all mine" she smiled.

And then she was gone.

A few moments later my friend woke up.

"Did I miss anything?" He enquired.

"Erm, not really" I lied as I tried to gather my thoughts together.

Shortly afterwards we said our goodbyes and rather than go straight home I decided to go for a walk in the park to ponder on what had just occurred. After a while I came across a bench and plonked myself down.

I thought back to what she had said: 'cease to look where I am not.' I began to think about my Grandfather who had passed away recently and it dawned on me that I had only been concerned with where he no longer was; I only ever looked at the void. As the realization started to sink in, I again had the sensation that I was not alone. I wasn't. My Grandfather sat next to me on the bench. This did not alarm me in any way, quite the opposite. The feeling of calm and peace that radiated from him was like the rays of the sun wrapping around me. We sat and chatted for what seemed like ages. He spoke of what he was doing and who he had seen, it was a truly remarkable and personal experience. When he left I knew with certainty that he would always be there for me.

As I was driving home, obviously, my thoughts were on the events of this extraordinary day. I had all sorts of questions running around in my head with no real answers, thoughts just kept churning around. Then I had an overwhelming feeling which arose from within me; I didn't need answers, I didn't need to understand. I had just witnessed something that had no understanding, it was the way it was, and it is the way it is.

Wow, I thought, I am really getting the hang of this! I am sailing through the training.

Just then I pulled up at some traffic lights and was waiting for them to change, when all of a sudden I had the strangest sensation, I experienced my nose. Seriously, I experienced my nose for the first time! I wasn't looking at it, or touching it; I was feeling it within me. That's the best and only way I can describe it. I sensed it in me, it was neither large nor small, long or thin, it was just perfect. It felt like perfection!

When I arrived home, I raced indoors and excitedly grabbed a pen and my notebook and wrote:

ME

My Nose – Perfect!
My Grief – Unnecessary

I sat contemplating the day and was feeling very smug with myself. I couldn't help thinking that I was making great progress and I could soon be near to completing the training.

Just then the telephone rang. It was a friend of mine whom I had not spoken to for a while. We got chatting and started to catch up on things and then she began to tell me about a mutual friend of ours and what she had been saying about me behind my back. It was not nice to hear. How could a so-called friend say such things? I was furious. When the call came to an end I was livid. What right has she to judge me? Who is she to say those things? All of these questions were running through my mind.

All night I tossed and turned. I was having imaginary conversations with the so-called friend. I was so upset I couldn't sleep. I also questioned why my other friend felt the need to tell me; did she also think those things about me? She knew it would hurt; why tell me, what was her motive? All of my training seemed to go out of the window – it was of no importance to me in this situation. I was too angry. Forget about loving all people, I wanted to throttle them both!

The following morning, I got up still angry and ready to fight (metaphorically of course). I switched on the computer as normal and the following message was in my inbox:

Internal Memorandum

Dear Trainee,

I notice that you are a little upset. Maybe you would like to consider the following:-

Believe nothing, no matter where you read it, or who said it, unless it agrees with your own reason and your own common sense. In addition, holding on to anger is like grasping a hot coal with the intent of throwing it at someone; you are the one who gets burned.

I am sure this will be of help.

Kindest regards,
B xx

As I sat and drank my coffee, I contemplated the e-mail. The words were like an arrow hitting my heart. The events of the previous night just melted away from my mind. There was nothing I needed to do.

4

SINK OR SWIM

I had not seen The Barefoot Indian for a while now and Head Office was very quiet, so I continued to plough my own furrow. As the weeks passed it was more evident that there were no rules or expectations, it was unlike any job I had ever had. I was my own boss!

The weather was gloriously hot so having done all my chores I decided to go for a swim. I went to the local pool expecting it to be very busy but I was surprised at how quiet it was. Brilliant! I can really go for it, no interruptions; I may even break my record and do seventy lengths, I thought to myself as I was getting changed.

The water was refreshing and I began to swim up and down, up and down. When I reached fifty lengths I started to feel the strain and stopped to catch my breath. I then felt I could go on after all, I only had another twenty lengths to go, I just needed to pull on my reserves. So off I went.

After a couple more lengths, I started to feel really heavy and was struggling to continue. I was just thinking about quitting when I began to sink. I desperately tried to get to the surface but the more I struggled the deeper I sank. I couldn't breathe; the water was filling my airways and panic set in. I was drowning. The more I tried to gasp for breath the more I felt as though I was suffocating. This is it I thought, the end.

Suddenly my chest started to expand and my breath seemed to

come alive, the panic stopped and a sense of peace came over me. I started to have the sensation that I was moving backwards. I was! I was moving inwards. I always believed that in death you leave the body but I was travelling within the body. I wasn't leaving the world, the world was leaving me. I started to feel free, unrestricted by the body. I felt as though I was growing, spreading, going beyond. I could no longer feel the water; all I could feel was light and space.

I looked around, the light was bright and there standing to the right of me, smiling, was The Barefoot Indian.

"What's going on? Am I dead?" I enquired.

"Well, if you are you look good on it," she laughed.

"Where am I?"

"You are seeing life from a different view," she replied.

"It looks wonderful, I feel so calm and still. I feel I can do anything; there seems to be nothing to limit me. This surely must be heaven?" I asked.

"It is," she replied.

I stood for a while and took in the surroundings. The air was fresh and clean so I took a deep breath and filled up my lungs. White doves were flying above me and around me; the movement of their wings blew a gentle breeze across my face. I was just thinking what a wonderful place this was when The Barefoot Indian's voice broke my thoughts.

"I'm glad you are here, there is something I would like to share with you."

She took me by the hand and led me through a gateway. We walked through the most beautiful landscaped garden and came across an ornate iron bench where we sat. The aroma from the flowers was divine.

"Your world is a web of thoughts and emotions," she said. "These thoughts and emotions have no purpose so you do not need to concern yourself with them."

"What do you mean?" I asked.

"I shall put it this way. The sun, the moon and the stars have a purpose. Every day they shine. They light the way. Nothing stops them shining. Each aspect is unique yet they work together as one and display a most beautiful and complex sight. The sun, the moon and stars are just doing what they do and just being what they are."

"Now, your thoughts and emotions are like the clouds. They come and go; they change form and can temporarily block the view of the sun, the moon and the stars. When the clouds obscure your view of the heavens, have the sun, the moon and the stars stopped shining?" she asked.

"Well, no" I replied.

"Can the presence of the clouds alter the sun, the moon and the stars? Do they have any power over them?"

"No, the heavens will always be there" I said.

She continued "So, we have the sun, the moon and the stars which in their simplicity are an awesome force that lights the way and cannot be altered and we have the clouds which come and go, change form and can dissolve in any moment. Which one should you be concerned with; that which is unalterable and permanent? Or your thoughts and emotions which are like the clouds, flimsy and temporary?"

"Well, there is no contest really. It's got to be that which is permanent" I answered.

"But how do I concern myself with the permanent?" I asked.

"By not being concerned with the temporary," she replied. I had a feeling she would say that, I thought to myself.

She continued, "When your attention is no longer on the temporary, it is automatically on the permanent."

"Yes, I can see that." I said. "But if my thoughts and emotions are temporary then what is permanent?"

"You are!" she said, smiling. "I shall leave that with you for you to think about."

We sat for a short while in silence and then The Barefoot Indian said,

"Before you go there is someone who would like to see you."

"What do you mean before I go? I thought I would be staying," I said.

"No, soon your attention will be back on 'the clouds' that which obscures," she replied.

"Great!" I said sarcastically.

She got hold of my hand again and led me from the garden. We had only walked a short distance when we arrived at the quaintest little cottage I had ever seen. It was just like a picture on a chocolate box, with the most colorful flowers planted in the garden bordered by a little picket fence. The cottage was located in a secluded part of a wood although strangely the trees didn't block out any light. As we approached the gate, I saw a person walking up to us from our left. As the person got nearer I suddenly realized who it was. It was a friend from the past who I had not seen for about five years.

"Chris!" I said. "What are you doing here?"

She looked different but I could not really put my finger on why.

"Hello," she said warily. "I have come to the cottage for a little rest, I really need to sleep for a while, I have been very tired lately. Please don't tell anyone I am here just yet."

"OK." I said, a little bemused.

Just then everything suddenly went dark and I felt like I was shrinking. When the sensation stopped after what seemed like ages, I opened my eyes. I was floating on my back in the middle of the swimming pool.

I'd better get out, I thought.

I quickly got dressed and headed home. I felt good, just a little light headed. When I arrived home, the first thing I did was to collect my notebook and pen and write:

ME

My Nose – Perfect!
My Grief – Unnecessary
My Breath – Alive

As I sat and pondered the most amazing events of the day, I noticed that my answer phone was flashing. I pushed the play button. "Hi it's me," said the voice. "I have some bad news. I'm sorry to have to tell you that Chris died in the early hours of this morning after a long battle with cancer."

5

PROFITS AND PROPHETS

I was really, really enjoying my new job even though I was still an apprentice. For the first time in my life I felt as though I had a purpose and each day brought a new experience. I was uncertain as to what the purpose was but I felt confident that I was heading in the right direction and that if the training continued in the way it was going I would soon get the promotion that was waiting for me.

However, there was just one little thing that was niggling me and that was money! I had yet to receive any wages and I had been using my savings to keep me going. My savings were disappearing fast and panic was starting to set in. I decided to contact Head Office to clarify the position. After what seemed like an eternity of waiting I finally got an e-mail.

Internal Memorandum

Dear Trainee,

Thank you for your enquiry regarding your wages. As previously mentioned regarding your position within this Company, the rewards will be beyond anything you can imagine.

Do not start worrying: 'Where will my food come from? Or my drink? Or my clothes? It is known that you need all these things. Instead, be concerned above everything else with the 'Unlimited' and what it requires of you. The 'Unlimited' will provide you with all these other things. So do not worry about tomorrow; it will have enough worries of its own. There is no need to add to the troubles each day brings.

Yours forever,
JC

What the hell did that mean? I thought. Will I receive a wage or what?

I decided to be a good student and take on board what was said rather than send another e-mail for clarification. I concluded that if I pushed my worry to one side everything would be given to me.

How wrong I was! Nothing came except more worry. The more I tried to push my worry away the bigger it got. My savings were almost gone and there was no indication that the 'Unlimited' was providing anything. It was time to consult with The Barefoot Indian.

I thought of her and waited for her to arrive but she did not come. I even shouted out loud for her but still she did not appear. This went on for days but to no avail. Finally, after about a week of panic and fear, she came.

"Thank God you have come," I said. "I have been asking for you all week."

"No you haven't" she replied. "You haven't been asking for me, you've been begging for me."

"Is that wrong?" I questioned sheepishly.

"You can never do wrong but your actions can reap very different results" she said.

"What do you mean?" I asked.

"If you stand in a dark room and ask me to give you light, that I can do because light is what I know. If you stand in a dark room and beg me to get rid of darkness, that I cannot do because I know nothing about darkness. So, which one would you like; do you want to know how to get light or do you want to know how to get rid of darkness?" she asked.

"I want to know how to get light," I replied.

"Correct answer" she said. "Now let's move on to money, the root of all evil! From where you stand it makes the world go around. From where I stand it brings it to a grinding halt."

"In what way?" I enquired.

"Money is an invention of man, a way to control and instill fear in people. The more money you have, the more power you have. The less money you have, the less power you have. Those with more can control those with less. If a Government had no money it would have no power, the two go hand in hand. Money is emotion; motives manifested."

She continued, "Money is not a living thing; it is what you do with it that gives it life. In your world it is believed that you cannot live without it. In my world you cannot live with it!"

"That's quite a tough thing to grasp," I said.

"It can appear to be tough because your belief in money rules you."

"For example, how do you feel when you have it?" she asked.

"Well, carefree I suppose because I feel secure. I love to shop till I drop, it makes me feel elated." I answered.

"And how do you feel when you haven't got any?" she asked.

"Fearful, life becomes a struggle, I worry all the time," I said.

"So you see it controls how you feel. How can you truly live when you are controlled, never free to be free?" she said.

"You can't," I answered. "But how do you stop being ruled by it?"

"By realizing that it doesn't rule you. It has no life. You give life to it."

She continued, "Allow me to ask you. How much does it cost per year to keep the sun shining? How much does a bird spend on food per year? What rent is charged to the rivers for crossing the land to the sea? How much does a tree charge the bee to take its pollen? How much are sheep charged for their winter coats?" She paused for me to answer.

"Well, nothing but that's nature," I said.

"Yes, it is nature, the natural. That which man has no power over and can never control. Nature is natural; it is being what it is and doing what it does. Look around you, the only thing that needs money is you! You say 'you can only have that if you give me this,' 'you can only have this if you give me that.'

"You need to question which came first, money or motive," she said.

"Motive, I guess" I replied.

"That's right, motive came first, so be without motives. You can rise above your motives at any time; that's down to you. Observe them, challenge them. It is your motives that are questionable; in truth your motives are the root of all evil!"

She continued, "Remember that which created nature created you also. Find your natural state; what applies to nature also applies to you. Everything nature needs is provided. If you look at the world and see the awesome, magnificent power that enables it to be; don't you think that that power has the ability to take care of you also?"

"Well, when you put it like that, it couldn't fail to take care of me. In fact it seems really stupid of me to think that I could do a better job of looking after myself!" I said.

"But what is that awesome, magnificent power?"

"You will know soon enough, the first step is to get used to allowing it to take care of you," she said.

"How do I do that?" I enquired.

"Well, I think you are now ready to take on a little challenge. If you are willing I suggest that tomorrow when you leave your house, you leave without any money or possessions. Only carry the clothes on your back and have no thought of where you are going or where you will end up. Be like the wind, nothing can stop it and everything yields to it. Are you up to the challenge?" she asked.

"Absolutely!" I replied.

"Very well," she said. "Good luck and remember, the only obstacles are in your own mind. Follow your heart not your head and enjoy!"

With that she left.

I went to bed excited about the challenge the following day. When I woke in the morning I had that sinking feeling that you get when you have agreed to something but you don't know exactly what.

I ate some breakfast, a huge one, just to be on the safe side, God knows when I would be eating again (actually he probably did!)

I got dressed, with layers, again just to be on the safe side (seven pairs of knickers do make your butt look big. Not recommended!) and made my way to the front door. OK, this is it, I thought as I walked out of the door.

Without thinking I made my way to the local town. Three miles I walked, but the weather was fine and the air was fresh so it felt very pleasant. I was very aware of all the birds busily building their nests and collecting food. How right The Barefoot Indian was, I thought, everything they need is there for them, and also as an afterthought, how strange the world would be if there were no birds.

I wandered around the town, looking in the shop windows, when suddenly a familiar voice called out to me from across the road. It was an ex colleague of mine who I had not seen for about six years.

"Hello, how are you?" I asked, really excited.

"Great," he replied. "Do you fancy a coffee? On me of course, and we can catch up on all the news."

"Sounds perfect," I said.

We entered a lovely, quaint tea room and ordered the drinks. A huge plate of toasted teacakes was placed on the table.

"I think there has been a mistake," I said to the waitress "we didn't order any teacakes."

"No, there's no mistake," she said, "you are our thousandth customer so we would like you to have your coffee and these teacakes with our complements. Enjoy."

"Thank you" I said whilst smiling to myself.

We tucked into the teacakes and started to catch up with each other. It emerged that he had moved to the Canary Islands and was now running a successful business out there. Sounds wonderful, I thought, as I ate the last teacake (stocking up again!)

"What about you," he asked, "what have you been up to?"

I proceeded to tell him about my new job and briefly outlined some of the experiences that had come my way.

"Wow," he said, "what a job!"

Then right out of the blue he asked, "How about coming out to the Canaries and inspiring some of my staff?"

"When?" I enquired.

"Tonight, I am flying back there tonight," he said.

I was just about to say no as I couldn't possibly go at such short notice. There was too much to organize and besides which I couldn't afford the flight, when I suddenly heard The Barefoot Indian's voice coming from deep within me: 'be like the wind.'

"I will pay for your flight and you can stay in one of my villas free of charge," my friend said. "Come on, what's to keep you here? We can go and get your passport now and then be on our way."

"OK, let's go," I said excitedly.

As I stood up to put on my coat, I was aware that there was something in the pocket. I felt inside and to my amazement I pulled out my passport. How on earth did that get there? I asked myself.

We arrived in the Canaries later that night. Stepping off the plane was like entering paradise, the heat was wonderful. We travelled by car for about thirty minutes and pulled up at the most magnificent villa that I had ever seen. We went inside, it was very spacious and the view from the patio doors overlooked the ocean.

"This is all yours for how ever long you require it" said my friend. "The fridge is full but should you require anything else or when you need to restock just let the housekeeper know what you need and she will get it for you, no need to pay, I'll sort all that out."

Surely I have died (again) and gone to heaven, I thought.

"When you feel ready, perhaps in a few days, come over to my offices and I shall introduce you to the staff and we will take it from there. OK?" he enquired.

"Great," I replied "although I am not quite sure what it is you want me to do with your staff."

"Inspire them," he said.

"But I am not really sure how to."

"Well, you inspired me by talking to me, so I guess you just need to talk to them," he said, "just go with the flow."

"I'll try" I said.

I went to bed, slept like a log and woke up in the morning in time to see the sun rising. How beautiful, what a wonderful place to be. As I watched the sun rise I did wonder what the bill would be like if the sun charged for giving its energy: the world would be bankrupt! It struck me in that moment that the sun never takes anything but only gives; that is all it can do. How cool, I thought, I'm starting to sound like The Barefoot Indian.

I had a wonderful time out there, no thoughts or worries; everything seemed to fall into place, from food to clothes, everything was provided.

I was introduced to some of the staff. I chatted to them without thinking about what I would say and the words just flowed from me. It was amazing to witness that when you give of yourself freely to others, they give more than enough back.

I think I achieved what was required, they seemed to be inspired and the sale figures increased within the company. Although that was not my objective, it did seem to make a difference; the members of staff were more relaxed and were enjoying what they were doing. I do remember a particular incident though; a guy came to me who was limping and asked me if I could do anything for his leg. Oh God, I thought, the dreaded healing thing again, maybe now I would be able to do it, just go with the flow, open your mouth and say something. So I did:

"Get up and walk," I said cringingly.

He did! But the only thing that happened was that he limped quicker as he walked out of the door. At some point I must ask The Barefoot Indian how it's done, I thought.

After a while of living it up and sunning myself, I had the feeling it was time to go home, no particular reason, I just felt that the time was right. It had been an amazing adventure but I was now ready for the next one.

Finally, after four months away I arrived home. I grabbed my notebook and pen and wrote:

<u>*ME*</u>

My Nose – Perfect!

My Grief – Unnecessary

My Breath – Alive

My Motives – Deceitful

My Pockets – Empty

My Wealth – Endless

I sat down for a while and thought about the challenge. I thought I did very well considering. There was just the little hiccup with the limping guy, but what the heck, I'm sure I still have a lot to learn.

I wondered how well Head Office thought I did. I switched on my computer and with some pride read the following e-mail.

Internal Memorandum

Dear Trainee,

Welcome home.

We are pleased that you enjoyed your challenge and would like to say that the awakened sages call a person wise when all his undertakings are free from anxiety about results.

Well done!

Yours truly,
K xx

I think there is a compliment in there somewhere.

6

ALL THINGS BRIGHT AND BEAUTIFUL

I continued to allow the awesome, magnificent power, the 'Unlimited,' to take care of me, though; at times this was not easy. The main problem was my own thoughts and emotions, there was a battle going on within me. Old habits die hard and when faced with a problem, not just financial, it was hard not to do what I would normally do and that was to react. I had to observe my own motives, thoughts and emotions, rise above them, see through them and allow the 'Unlimited' to take over. After all, the only thing that came between me and the 'Unlimited' was me!

It was during one of my particular battles, when I was winning and the 'Unlimited' was losing, that The Barefoot Indian appeared.

"Hello," she said, "having a good day?"

"No," I replied. "I feel so out of touch with everything, I seem to have no clarity and the 'Unlimited' is nowhere to be seen. In fact, I am doubting whether it exists at all."

"Oh dear," she smiled, undisturbed. "Why can you not see the 'Unlimited'?"

"I don't know," I said. "I guess it's hiding itself from me. Perhaps it is making me work hard in order to find it!"

"The 'Unlimited' can never hide, it is always on view for all to see," she said.

"Well, I don't see it!" I cried.

"Perhaps it is what you are looking through that is the problem," she said.

"What do you mean?" I asked.

"Let's put it this way. If you are looking at a wonderful view through a pair of binoculars and the binoculars are out of focus, what will you see?" she asked.

"A blur," I replied.

"And does that mean the view is blurred or just your view of it?"

"Just my view of it," I said.

"So, the only thing to do is change the focus and everything becomes clear?" she questioned.

"Yes," I replied.

"And who can change the focus?" she asked.

"The one holding the binoculars," I said.

"So, the view cannot do anything about the way you view it, only the one looking can change what they see?" she said.

"Yes," I agreed.

"And so it is with the 'Unlimited,' always on show but it is down to the one who's looking that determines how they see it," she concluded.

I thought about this for a while and then said

"If God, the 'Unlimited' or whatever you want to call it, is always on view for all to see, then I am only ever looking at God, the 'Unlimited' but in a distorted way?"

"Correct," she answered "You are learning fast."

Feeling much calmer and with a new outlook I started to prepare lunch for us both. It was a lovely day so we sat out in the garden to eat it. Everything seemed perfect and very still and I started to feel alive once again. As we sat I began to look around and nature was busy being itself, continuously, never ending, and always moving. I was contemplating life when The Barefoot Indian interrupted my thoughts.

"Now that you have started to re-focus your binoculars to see the 'Unlimited' would you like to hear the 'Unlimited'?" she asked.

"Of course I would," I answered. "How do I do that?"

"You have to start by listening" she said.

"Well that seems obvious!" I exclaimed.

"It is not as obvious as it sounds," she continued. "You are only used to hearing with your ears. The 'Unlimited' can only be heard through your heart."

"Right," I said waiting eagerly for her to continue.

"To listen through your heart, you have to go beyond all logic, beyond the rational," she said.

"OK," I said "how do I do that?"

Just as I asked that, the wind really whipped up as if from nowhere, it was quite strong, strong enough for the trees to sway. I wonder where that came from, it wasn't forecasted, I thought to myself.

"I'll show you," continued The Barefoot Indian. "Firstly, everyone and all things are the 'Unlimited' whether you agree or not, that is the way it is. To you, in your world, there is the living and the inanimate. In my world there is only the living."

"Let's take the wind for example, have you ever heard it speak?" she asked.

"Of course not" I replied. "It can't, can it?"

"You tell me," she said. "To make this a little easier for you I will pose a question to the wind. I will pose the question so that you have no preconceived ideas about it and consequently you will have no preconceived ideas about the answer. Besides which, the question I will ask only your heart can answer."

"Are you ready?" she asked.

"Er, yes," I said with some uncertainty.

"OK, here we go" she said, "and remember, listen with your heart not your mind."

With that she stood up and yelled to the wind "Wind, where do you come from?"

Well she was right, there was no way I could answer that with logic unless I had a degree in meteorology!

I sat and waited, silently and calmly. I pushed all thoughts and expectations from my mind. I waited and waited and then all of a sudden a voice, a deep voice, arose up from within me and from outside of me and said:

"I come from where I am going to!"

"Wow" I said, "that's amazing, I don't understand it, but it's amazing. That truly came from the wind!"

"That's right, it did," said The Barefoot Indian.

The wind suddenly dropped and everything was calm again. I rushed indoors to get a drink to calm my excitement and to go to the loo before returning to The Barefoot Indian. I wanted to know more, this was a breakthrough, unbelievable! What was more unbelievable was when I stepped through the door to return to the garden there was three inches of snow and it was falling fast. What the hell is going on, I thought, the weather's gone mad, it's summer for goodness sake! Through the blizzard I saw The Barefoot Indian, smiling and laughing as I approached her.

"Ready for the next one?" she said.

"What next one?" I enquired.

"The next question," she replied. "This time you can hear what the snow has got to say!"

This is barmy, I thought, but somehow it seemed perfectly natural.

"OK, let's do it," I said.

"Same again, I'll pose a question to the snow and you wait for the answer," she said.

"You're in charge," I said.

With that she stood up and shouted to the snow, "Snow, what is your experience?"

Again I sat and waited patiently but this time a little longer, partly because I kept being distracted by the snow hitting me, cold and wet on my face. Then all of a sudden the deep voice came from within and without.

"Warmth, that is what I experience," said the snow. Again, this seemed weird but the answers were undeniable and could not have come from my logic, it was beyond that. With the answers came a feeling, it was like the answers were feelings and the feelings were answers.

"How are you feeling?" asked The Barefoot Indian.

"Great," I said. "I'm starting to feel at one, an affinity with everything!"

With that the snow stopped pouring from the sky and melted from the ground quicker than I had ever seen before. Within a few moments the weather was back to how it should be in summer.

"Would you like another one, just to make sure?" she asked.

Oh God, I thought to myself, what are we going to get now, thunder, lightning, or a typhoon perhaps?

"Yes please, but can it be other than the weather?" I asked.

"No problem," she answered. "I shall ask your house a question."

"My house?" I enquired, "I can just about understand nature talking, but a house, that is nothing more than bricks and mortar."

"I have heard of Doctor Doolittle who talks to the animals but what do you call someone who talks to their house? The House Doctor perhaps?" I said jokingly.

"Everything is God in God's world, everything is the 'Unlimited'" she said.

"OK, here we go," she continued.

She turned to face my house, held her arms outstretched and shouted, "House, what lives in you?"

I waited and it was not long this time before the deep voice arose from within and without. This time, however, the voice was louder and more powerful than the previous times.

"Love lives in me," said the house.

After a few moments of standing there in silence and coming to terms with what I had just experienced my attention was drawn back to the wonderful Barefoot Indian.

"How was that?" she asked.

"Amazing, extraordinary!" I replied. "Even though it seems a little crazy, it was perfectly natural and the voice I heard was more real than any voice I have heard in my life."

"So it is," she said.

"What have you concluded from this little exercise?" she continued.

"Well, I would have to say that the awesome, magnificent power, God, the 'Unlimited' is truly all things. All is truly bright and beautiful," I answered.

"So it is," she said again.

"In silence you hear everything," I concluded.

We made our way back indoors. What a day, I thought, I wonder what's next? The Barefoot Indian was preparing to go when she turned to me and asked,

"Oh, before I go, wasn't there something you would like to ask me about healing?"

"No, no," I lied "it's never entered my head."

As with any job there is always something that you dislike and this was going to be my pet hate, I don't know why, it's just one of those things. I wondered whether I could get all the way without doing any healing. I'll try, I thought.

"Very well," she said. "Bye for now."

"Bye," I said, "and thank you."

Then she was gone.

I sat down and went through the events of the day in my mind when my computer interrupted my thoughts:

"You have new mail," it said in a techno sort of voice.

Internal Memorandum

Dear Trainee,

Please take a moment to reflect on today.

Today you were given what the eye has not seen, what the ear has not heard and what the hand has not touched.

He who experiences the unity of life sees his own Self in all beings and all beings in his own Self and looks on everything with an impartial eye.

Congratulations!

From all at Head Office,
Xx

I decided to have a bath and reflect on the day, but before I went upstairs I picked up my notebook and wrote:

ME

My Nose – Perfect!
My Grief – Unnecessary
My Breath – Alive
My Motives – Deceitful
My Pockets – Empty
My Wealth – Endless
My Vision – Clear
My Mind – Redundant
My Heart – Open
My Hearing – Alert

7

IS THAT YOUR FINAL ANSWER?

It dawned on me that if I should ever pass the exam and achieve the promotion to Messiahress then surely, in my new position, I would be asked a whole range of questions by people who would come my way. I thought it sensible to compile a list of the type of questions that I may be asked in the future and pose them to The Barefoot Indian, just to get some sense of what's involved and what the answers were likely to be. I was being very efficient and prided myself on that.

She arrived at my request. I explained what my thoughts were and asked if she was willing to answer some or all of the questions.

"Of course," she said, smiling. "I'll do anything to help, just start when you are ready."

"OK, here goes," I said.

Me: "What is the meaning of life?"

TBFI: "Whatever meaning you wish to give it."

Me: "What is the purpose of life?"

TBFI: "Whatever purpose you wish to give it."

Me: "Why do we die?"

TBFI: "You don't."

Me: "Why are we born?"

TBFI: "You were not."

Me: "Why is there suffering?"

TBFI: "There can be no suffering when you know the one who is suffering."

Me: "I am always failing in life, why?"

TBFI: "You only fail to be what you are not. Rejoice."

Me: "Where is heaven?"

TBFI: "Wherever you want it to be."

Me: "How do I get rich?"

TBFI: "By knowing your worth."

Me: "Why am I always poor?"

TBFI: "Because you are not rich."

Me: "Can the sick be well?"

TBFI: "Can the well be sick?"

I paused.

"I shall have to stop," I said. "I can't continue with these questions."

"Why not?" she asked, surprised.

"Because the answers are like slogans you would find on a tee shirt, I don't think that these are the answers that people would want. They are like riddles!" I said.

"Perhaps it's the questions that are riddles," she replied.

"There you go again!" I said. "Are there no straight answers to any questions?"

"Perhaps there are no questions," she said.

"Of course there are questions, lots of them," I said.

"Well then, where are all the answers?" she enquired, laughing.

"I DON'T KNOW! I said.

"Look" she said "A river will travel miles and miles over terrain to get to the sea, the source. On its journey it encounters many obstacles, from fallen trees to narrowing riverbanks, from boulders to dams. It flows around them, through them or over them, nothing stops it flowing to its destination, it is on a mission. Imagine what would happen if the river stopped and questioned all of these things, if it tried to sort them out along its way. The sea would be empty! The river cannot be stopped by anything. So it is with life, you are on a mission, heading to a destination and nothing can stop you. Be like the river, heading to the source without question."

"Well, when you put it like that," I said.

Again, her words hit my heart like an arrow.

"Can I ask just one more question?" I asked.

"Yes."

"Why do you and everyone at Head Office speak with analogies, parables or stories?" I questioned.

"Because only your heart can understand them, your mind cannot," she replied.

I thought to myself, is that another tee shirt slogan? But somehow I guessed it was not.

When she left, I wrote in my notebook:

> ## ME
>
> My Nose – Perfect!
> My Grief – Unnecessary
> My Breath – Alive
> My Motives – Deceitful
> My Pockets – Empty
> My Wealth – Endless
> My Vision – Clear
> My Mind – Redundant
> My Heart – Open
> My Hearing – Alert
> My Mouth – Silent

I woke up the next morning to the sound of the post dropping through the letter box. I got up and went downstairs to collect the mail. There was a small package, wrapped in brown paper with the franking stamp from Head Office printed along the top. What could this be? I thought as I eagerly opened it.

I pulled out the letter first which read:

Internal Memorandum

Dear Trainee,

We couldn't help overhearing your conversation with the beautiful Barefoot Indian yesterday.

We have therefore sent you an early Christmas present, just to demonstrate that even as you wander through your daily life, there will always be something there to guide you to the 'Unlimited.'

We are sure you will find this useful in more ways than one!

With our very best wishes,

From us all at Head Office,
Xx

P.S. 'Wear' there's a will there's a way.

How sweet of them I thought and I couldn't help but laugh out loud when I pulled out the gift. It was a tee shirt of the highest quality with the following printed on it:

Ponderisms!

- Don't be ruled by that which doesn't rule you
- Only give what all can receive
- What you desire you cannot have, what you have can never be desired
- Freedom is knowing of no such thing
- Signposts are not the destination
- In the midst of illusion you'll find 'u'
- You cannot be something without being everything
- Your life _is_ a meditation

PARTY POOPER

I decided to go for a walk, a long walk, as there didn't seem to be much going on. Things had gone very quiet on the training front and I was starting to feel a little bored. A walk would clear my head and hopefully bring about the next step, I thought to myself as I set off.

As I was walking my mind began to wander and I remembered the day that I went to Head Office. The words of JC came back to me: 'once you have decided to walk this path you will not be able to get off it.' I wondered why he had said that.

As there had been a definite lack of challenges recently, I decided to create one of my own. I shall try to get off 'the path,' I thought

With a spring in my step I continued my walk, planning how I would get off 'the path.' It was not that I particularly wanted to get off it; I just saw it as a challenge. In order to fully understand what JC meant, I saw it as an opportunity to find out for myself.

I thought that the best way to go about this task was to do something that I used to do on a regular basis, absorb myself in it and ignore everything that had happened subsequently. I therefore decided to hold a dinner party and invite about fifteen people whom I had not seen for a long time.

The day of the party arrived, so I got up early as there was quite a lot to do. I made the conscious effort to push all thoughts of the training out of my mind and be as 'normal' as I used to be. I set about preparing for the evening and was amazed that I wasn't panicking. I used to be a nervous wreck whenever I held a dinner party in the past, worrying about how the food would turn out and praying that I did not overcook anything, but this time it didn't bother me, I felt calm, stress-free and had a feeling of certainty that everything would be perfect.

As I was doing this as a challenge I was desperate to get back my old feelings of stress but no matter how many dreadful scenarios I imagined in my head as to what could happen at a dinner party, I remained as calm as a duck pond. Maybe it was the soothing sound of Elvis coming through my CD player that was calming me or maybe I was already beginning to fail the task.

I was waiting for my guests to arrive when I couldn't help but notice the most magnificent sunset through the kitchen window. I stood there watching it in all its glory, the sky was full of reds and pinks and Elvis was playing in the background, what more could a girl want I thought.

My guests arrived and it was wonderful to see them all. The wine began to flow and the house was soon filled with chatting and laughter, the more the wine flowed the louder the noise became. As I did the final preparations with the food, the noise was already beginning to grate on me but I pushed this to one side and began to serve the food.

We sat around the table and started to eat. The food was done to perfection, no disasters this time! The conversation began to wane as my guests tucked in to the food. I suddenly remembered the sunset.

"Did anyone see the wonderful sunset this evening?" I enquired.

"No," was the answer in unison.

One of my friends continued, "I haven't got time to watch a sunset; there are far more important things to do than to stand around watching the sky."

Everyone laughed and was in agreement with this.

"Just out of curiosity," I said, "how many sunsets have you seen in your life?" I threw this question out to anyone who was willing to answer.

"I don't know," "Wouldn't have a clue," "I can't remember seeing any," was the consensus.

This conversation was quickly dropped and moved on to the usual 'he said, she said' stuff. I took a back seat and began to observe my friends who were getting more and more animated about all the gossip and back stabbing that was going on. They were constantly judging people, but it seemed to me that the only power their judgments had was the power they gave to them.

I went to make coffee and couldn't get from my mind that none of them had taken the time to watch a sunset. How could they not see or want to see something so magnificent, I thought; they seemed so concerned with their own little worlds that they had no time to reflect on the real world.

I went back into the room with the coffee and they were busy chatting about what they had achieved, what they hoped to achieve, where they were heading. I desperately tried to join in the conversation, but to no avail. I felt like I was an outcast, not because of them but because of me. I suddenly couldn't find a place for myself in their worlds.

I continued to observe them and it dawned on me that all of their conversations were about something that wasn't present. They would only talk about someone that wasn't there, they would describe an event that had passed away and they spoke about their future dreams and plans. Not one of them spoke of, or could see, that which was present. The conversations seemed to be of no importance to anyone other than themselves. I could see that their lives were full of hopes and fears. It was like they were on some kind of imaginary train journey, not knowing where they had come from and not knowing where they were heading. Along the way they were collecting baggage, not just their own but others' as well, they were becoming heavy and burdened, but they didn't seem to mind. They had put all of their trust in the train driver who could be taking them anywhere and they were laughing along the way. Why don't they just get off?

Why don't they find their own way?

The music was becoming louder and their voices were trying to compete with it so I retreated outside to the garden.

The moon was shining down on me and lit up the garden in a silvery subtle light, in the far distance I could just make out a figure heading towards me. It was my trusted friend The Barefoot Indian.

"Having fun?" she asked.

"Not really," I replied, very relieved to see her. "I really tried to be 'normal' tonight but I found it impossible. I love my friends dearly but I feel as though we are on different planets now."

"Not different planets," she said "just different trains."

"What do you mean?" I asked.

"You jumped off the train to nowhere and started driving the train to everywhere," she said.

"How very true," I said, "but my friends must think I am a real party pooper."

"Don't be concerned with what others think. Be like the moon that cares not what you think of it, be like the sun which does not cry if you ignore it and be like the stars that will not change for you even if you dislike their display," she said. "The only thing that matters to them is to be."

Just as she said that an owl swooped down from the roof of the house to a nearby tree. It glided so gracefully, almost as if in slow motion, and looked so serene it took my breath away.

"What a fantastic sight," I said. "Who or what created such a magnificent creature?"

"Nothing created it," she said "it just is what it is."

"Don't be so obsessed with wanting to know where things come from. It blinds you to what is."

"What do you mean?" I asked again.

"When you looked at the owl, you were looking for that which created it. Your thoughts were on that and not on the bird." She continued, "Look at the bird without thought or judgment. See the bird and you might just find the answer you were looking for."

"I'll have to think about that one!" I said.

The owl took flight again and as it did it dropped a white feather from its wing. I watched as the feather gracefully and gently fell to the ground. I went over to pick up the feather and was disappointed to find that it had fallen into a dirty puddle. I fished out the feather from the puddle and looked at it in its limp and dirty state.

"What a shame," I said, "it's dirty, it's ruined."

"But is it not still a white feather?" asked The Barefoot Indian. "Underneath the dirt, what is there?"

"A white feather," I replied.

"And so it is with you, no matter how black things appear to be, you will always find that which is pure underneath," she said.

What a wonderful way to put it, I thought, I am like the white feather. I just need to get rid of the dirt!

I then turned to her and said, "I guess I have failed the task I set myself. JC was right, once you start to walk the path you cannot get off it."

"If you have just experienced failure," she said, "I can't wait to see what you experience when you succeed!"

I returned to the party and my friends had not noticed that I had briefly left. After a short while the wine ran out so the party ended and all my friends went home, having had a wonderful time. I started to clear away and clean up the house when I heard the 'techno' voice of my computer telling me I had new mail. I went over to the computer and read the following message:

Internal Memorandum

Dear Trainee,

There are only two mistakes one can make along the path to truth; not going all the way and not starting.

Lots of Love

B xx

I went to bed, took my notebook and pen with me and just before dropping off to sleep I wrote:

ME

My Nose – Perfect!
My Grief – Unnecessary
My Breath – Alive
My Motives – Deceitful
My Pockets – Empty
My Wealth – Endless
My Vision – Clear
My Mind – Redundant
My Heart – Open
My Hearing – Alert
My Mouth – Silent
My Judgments – Powerless
My Favorite Question – What do you mean?

FULL STEAM AHEAD

After failing the task I set myself and realizing that there was no way to get off the path, there was really only one option for me and that was to get to the destination as quickly as possible. There was no point in looking back, I could only go forward. With a new keenness to progress to the promotion I called upon The Barefoot Indian to help me speed things up.

"Hello," she said as she entered the room.

"Hi," I said.

"So you have decided to go full steam ahead?" She asked.

"Well yes, if that is possible," I replied.

"Everything is possible," she smiled. "Why the sudden change of heart?"

"Doing the task that I set myself caused me to think over my life. Before I applied for the job, my life was a struggle, nothing seemed to work out. It was as if I was on some kind of emotional treadmill, just when I thought I was getting somewhere something would come along and knock me back. The harder I tried the less successful I was and I was totally reliant on and influenced by others. I never realized to what extent just how miserable and painful my life was. I can now see that my life reflected whatever view I had of myself. That way of life holds no interest for me now, it's as if it never existed, the things I used to cling to, which I relied on to give me experiences, have disappeared and life has started to become full. I want to know that which makes all life possible and experience all that it has to offer."

"Very well," she said "where would you like to start?"

"I'm not sure," I said "I thought you could give me a guiding light."

"OK," she said "Let's go for a bike ride."

"A bike ride?" I exclaimed.

Of all the things that she could have come up with, a bike ride! That was the last thing I would ever think of as a path to enlightenment.

"Yes, let's go for a bike ride," she continued. "You live in such a beautiful area it would be nice to do some exploring."

"But I haven't got a bike," I said.

"No problem, I've brought them with me."

"But the weather is not very good, I saw the forecast this morning and it is going to rain later," I said.

"And do you believe that to be true?" she asked.

"Well, yes, maybe," I replied.

"And do you know that to be true?" she asked.

"What do you mean?" I enquired.

"What you believe to be true and what you know to be true are not the same," she continued. "You can believe that it is going to rain and it may or may not, or, you can know that it is not going to rain and it will not."

I pondered this for a moment and then said, "You'll have to leave that one with me."

"OK," she said. "Come on, let's go. We can have a picnic as well."

"Have a picnic? I haven't got any food in with which to prepare a picnic," I said.

"Do you have any more limitations you would like to place on yourself before we go?" she asked.

"What do you mean?" I asked once again.

"Well, I suggested that we do something today and you have spent all of your time coming up with obstacles which would have you believe that you cannot do what you want to do. All your thoughts are saying 'I can't because...' You are trying to place limitations on the 'Unlimited.' Why?" she asked.

"I don't know," I replied "I hadn't noticed that I was doing that."

"You are like the ocean trying to squeeze itself into a one inch pipe and no matter how painful that is, you argue for the limitation. Why? Your vastness is apparent and knows no bounds, you are free to ebb and flow across the world, unchallenged and free," she said.

"You are so right," I said. "Let's go."

We walked outside and to my surprise, standing on the driveway was a tandem bike. It was obviously brand new as the paintwork was immaculate and the wheel spokes were sparkling in the sun.

"Why did you bring a tandem?" I asked.

"I thought it would be fun," she replied. "You go at the front and lead the way. After all, you know the area better than me. Besides which it is always better to lead than to follow."

We mounted the tandem and off we went. It was strange at first but we soon got the hang of it. God knows what we must have looked like. A Barefoot Red Indian and someone who looked as though she had been squeezed into a one inch pipe!

The weather was strangely perfect for a bike ride; it was neither too hot nor too cold. The birds were singing, the sky was blue and the air was pure. I had the sense that I was living in another world but had not gone anywhere.

The ride took us around some beautiful countryside and in some places it was quite hilly. This was challenging for any bike rider and I found these hills quite difficult. They caused me to puff and pant and my skin began to glow. On arriving at the top of one particular hill I needed to stop to catch my breath, it was then that I noticed The Barefoot Indian was not in anyway breathless and looked as beautiful as ever.

"How do you do that?" I asked.

"Do what?" she replied.

"Not get out of breath."

"I am the breath," she said.

"Again, you will have to leave that one with me," I said.

We continued on our journey. We had been cycling for about three hours when I suddenly felt hungry.

"I am hungry," I said "shall we get something to eat at the next village?"

"No, we can stop here and go sit by that stream over there," she said pointing over a wall.

"But there are no shops around here," I said.

"There you go again, trying to limit the 'Unlimited' she said as she was climbing over the wall.

I followed her and we sat down by the stream.

"What would you like to eat?" she asked.

"Fish and chips," I replied rather sarcastically.

Fish and chips was the least likely meal to be available in the middle of a field. Wild mushrooms and watercress maybe, but fish and chips, no way!

"OK," she said, "just be patient while we wait."

I decided not to question her. She had a habit of making things work out so I assumed that this time would be no different. I was fascinated to see what would develop.

We sat by the stream. I watched it for a while flowing by on its way to its destination. I was mesmerized by the movement. I found myself thinking about the stream. I followed its journey in my mind – it started as a trickle, then became a stream, then became a river and finally it became the sea. It was always growing, expanding and gathering more of itself along the way. Perhaps that is what I am like? I questioned to myself.

I brought myself back to reality and checked to see if the food had arrived. I looked around but I couldn't see any. To pass the time I asked The Barefoot Indian.

"Where is heaven?"

"Heaven is everywhere," she replied.

"Then why don't I see it?"

"Because you imagine that you see something else."

"What do you mean?" I asked yet again.

"Your world is made up of duality. There is you and there is everything around you. You separate yourself from what you see. You see two when there is only ever one. Heaven is when you see all things as one," she replied.

She continued, "Take a look at the tandem, what do you see? Describe it to me."

"Well, I see two bikes joined together," I said.

"There, you said it, two bikes joined together. The reality is it has never been two bikes and never will be, it has always been one bike, one unit and always will be."

"But how does that equate to my life?" I asked.

"Your life is like a painting and in that painting there are many characters. All the characters in the painting are individual and unique. As you look at them there are some you like and some you dislike, you make distinctions between them and get lost in those distinctions."

I agreed.

"If you stand back from the painting and observe it rather than getting lost in the detail, what strikes you about it? What do you see?"

"I'm not sure," I said after thinking about it for a while.

"Everything on the canvas is paint. All the characters, the scenery and the scenario are made up of paint. Everything in the painting is paint. There are no distinctions; they are all paint. How can you judge anything when everything is from the same source, the one source? Heaven is when you see this," she concluded.

I sat and thought about this for a while, when all of a sudden my thoughts were interrupted by The Barefoot Indian.

"Lunch has arrived," she said.

I gathered my thoughts and came back to the present moment. I couldn't believe what was in front of me – fish and chips.

"Where did those come from?" I asked.

"Where do you think?" she said. "You must have heard of this: 'ask and you will receive; seek and you will find; knock and the door will be opened to you. For everyone who asks will receive and anyone who seeks will find and the door will be opened to him who knocks?"

"Yes I have," I said. "So what are you saying? All I need to do is ask?"

"Yes. Try it now," she said.

"What shall I ask for?" I enquired.

"You decide, but it is always a good thing to know what to ask for before you ask," she said.

"OK, I have thought of something," I said, "but I would prefer to keep it a secret, just in case it doesn't come."

She rolled her eyes upwards, sighed and said, "very well, if you must."

"If it doesn't come then you have not asked correctly" she stated.

"How do you ask correctly?" I asked.

"That is for you to find out. Practice makes perfect."

We sat and ate our fish and chips out of the paper.

"Why did we not get plates?" I asked.

"It is a picnic!" she said. "What did you expect?"

The fish and chips were wonderful, complete with salt and vinegar; they were the best I had ever eaten. After lunch we set off again on the tandem to make our way home. It had been a perfect day and of course there was no rain!

What I asked for never appeared.

When we arrived back home I invited The Barefoot Indian in for a drink but she declined.

"I have to go now," she said, "but before I go I will leave you with something to consider."

"The bike ride today has reflected the process of your life."

"In what way?" I asked.

"You have travelled many miles today to get to your destination but you were at the destination before you started the journey. Think about this."

"I will," I promised.

With that she moved to the front of the tandem and pedalled off looking as stunning as she did when she arrived that morning.

I wonder where she is going I thought to myself.

I slumped down on the sofa exhausted from all the pedalling and fresh air. I had learnt so much from today but felt that I had a lot more to learn by contemplating the events.

I was feeling incredibly relaxed and I could feel my eyes closing, but before nodding off on the sofa I wrote in my notebook and quickly checked my e-mail messages:

ME

My Nose – Perfect!

My Grief – Unnecessary

My Breath – Alive

My Motives – Deceitful

My Pockets – Empty

My Wealth – Endless

My Vision – Clear

My Mind – Redundant

My Heart – Open

My Hearing – Alert

My Mouth – Silent

My Judgments – Powerless

My Favorite Question – What do you mean?

My Opinions – Limiting

My Butt – Sore!

Internal Memorandum

Dear Trainee,

I trust that you had the most marvellous day and enjoyed your lunch immensely. I know that you have much to consider but I thought I would send you a little reminder.

In the sky there is no distinction between east and west; people create distinctions out of their own minds and then believe them to be true.

Unity can only be manifested by the Binary. Unity itself and the idea of Unity are already two.

Sleep well,
Love from B xx

10

LAST ORDERS PLEASE!

Things were definitely moving on at quite a pace. I felt as though I was waking up from a deep sleep. Life was fun, the nightmare was ending. My desire to learn was increasing each day and I entered in to the challenges with an open heart and without expectation. My life was becoming peaceful and worry was a distant memory. I had not looked in a mirror since the beginning but I could say with some certainty that I was beautiful; I could feel the beauty within me.

My only stumbling block was the 'asking'. I asked until I was blue in the face but to no avail; whatever I asked for it didn't come. I asked with please and thank you but this made no difference. I remembered The Barefoot Indian's words: 'if it doesn't come then you are not asking correctly.' Well I certainly wasn't asking correctly. I even tried sitting crossed legged or kneeling down as if to pray, no matter how I asked it did not make a difference. It was time to consult with The Barefoot Indian.

She didn't come straight away, I think to demonstrate a point, but she came a few days later as I was walking in the park.

"Hello," she said as she came up from behind me.

"Hi, how are you?" I asked, very pleased to see her.

"Perfect," she answered.

Of course she is I thought, how stupid of me to ask.

"I am really struggling with the 'asking' thing." I continued. "It just doesn't seem to work for me."

"I'm sure that is not true, what makes you different?" she said.

"It's all in the way you ask."

"So I gather, but my way is obviously incorrect," I exclaimed.

She progressed "Let me give you a nudge in the right direction. Why does a child ask its mother for food, or pocket money, or even help?"

"Because the child knows the mother will provide all of those things," I said.

"That's right, but why can she provide all of those things?" she asked.

I thought about it as we walked around the lake. My mind was blank. As we were walking and not talking, I suddenly saw a mother and child throwing bread to the ducks; it was then that the answer came. They could only give bread to the ducks if they had bread to give.

"I think I've got it!" I suddenly said. "The mother can only provide all those things because she has them to give."

"Excellent," she said. "She can only provide what she has to give and the child only asks for what it knows the mother can give."

"Now, tell me one thing that you have asked for," she said.

"Well, on the day of the picnic I asked for an apple," I said, a little embarrassed.

"And when you asked did you know that the 'Unlimited' had an apple to give?"

"No, to be honest, I never really thought about it," I replied.

"So you asked for an apple without knowing if it could be given or even if it had it to give."

"Yes," I said, "but surely I would only know it had an apple to give when I received it?"

"Common error," she said. "With your approach you were uncertain whether it had an apple to give so all you saw was your doubt, your unknowingness, an empty space. You got what you asked for. Know that the 'Unlimited' is unlimited there is nothing it cannot give, and then ask. The results are very different."

She continued "If a mother will give her child everything

that she has to give how much more will the 'Unlimited' give to you?"

"It will give me anything," I said. "Anything I could ask for."

"Well then, ask now," she said, "and remember, only ask for what you know can be given. Instinct will tell you when you have asked properly."

"OK," I said. I closed my eyes and accepted with all my heart that there is nothing the 'Unlimited' cannot give. It has all to give. I thought of what I wanted and knew that it had it to give. I knew with certainty that I would receive what I had asked for. I opened my eyes and looked down at my hands and there it was, an orchid, exactly as I had asked.

"Brilliant!" she said. "Now let's move on."

We continued our walk around the lake. We were not speaking but I noticed that we were talking. I could hear her and she could hear me but our lips didn't move.

"What is heaven?" I asked.

"Knowing there is no such thing as hell," she replied. "Hell is in your mind only."

"What do you mean?" I enquired.

"Your thoughts deny your very being, they speak of what you are not," she said. "It is like you are asleep and dream all sorts of things. Whilst asleep you have nightmares, you find yourself in different situations, some pleasant some not so. In a moment you can wake up to the reality that you are safely tucked up in bed, warm, snug and secure. Upon waking and realizing where you are and that your thoughts were but a dream, you are in heaven; that is what heaven is."

There was nothing I could add to this.

"Come on" she said. "let's have a paddle in the lake."

"A paddle?" I said, "Are you mad? The water will be freezing at this time of year!"

"Why do you say that?" she asked. "Do you believe that to be true or do you know that to be true?"

"Point taken," I said.

With that she ran into the lake.

"Come on in, it's lovely and warm," she said.

I followed her and she was right, it was warm. She then scooped some of the water into her hand and started to drink it.

"What are you doing?" I exclaimed. "That water is filthy!"

"No it's not," she said "it's lovely, come and have a drink."

She held out her hands for me to take a sip. I closed my eyes so as not to see the dirty water, it would put me off. With total trust in her I took a sip of the water. It went down my throat, I was amazed, it was lovely, it was wine!

"That's wine," I said.

"I know," she said. "It's an Oldie but Goldie, it never fails to amaze people."

"How did you do that?" I asked.

"There is no 'how'," she said.

"What do you mean?"

"Let me ask you, can you walk across this lake?" she asked.

"Probably not."

"Why not?" she asked.

"Well, because I would sink!" I said.

"Who says so?"

"Me."

"And why do you say that?"

I thought about this for a while.

"I don't know, I just do," I finally concluded.

"So, you really believe that you cannot walk across this lake and can't turn it into wine."

"Yes, I believe that to be true," I said.

"Well then, you need to deal with that which says you can't," she said. "Whatever you say is true, will be so."

She continued, "If for a moment you doubt your theories, another reality will be waiting for you."

"So I don't need to know how to do it, I only need to remove that from within me that says I can't do it?" I said. "And then, if I say I can do it, I will?"

"Correct," she said.

We continued our paddle and drank some more wine, quite a bit more actually. We were having so much fun that I didn't want it to end. I began to practice what I had learnt but I think I had had too much to drink; I could barely stand up in the water let alone walk across it!

After a while I decided to go home. I needed my bed. But before we parted company I gave my orchid to The Barefoot Indian as we said our goodbyes.

I was too drunk to contemplate anything that evening but I did manage to grab my notebook and write the following before collapsing in a heap:

> *ME*
>
> *My Nose – Perfect!*
> *My Grief – Unnecessary*
> *My Breath – Alive*
> *My Motives – Deceitful*
> *My Pockets – Empty*
> *My Wealth – Endless*
> *My Vision – Clear*
> *My Mind – Redundant*
> *My Heart – Open*
> *My Hearing – Alert*
> *My Mouth – Silent*
> *My Judgments – Powerless*
> *My Favorite Question – What do you mean?*
> *My Opinions – Limiting*
> *My Butt – Sore!*
> *My Face – Beautiful*
> *My Thinking – Wrong*
> *My Ability – Amazing*
> *My Feet – Can walk on water*
> *My Room – Spinning!*

I woke up the next morning, with a little hangover. A small card was sitting on the door mat:

Get well soon

Dear Trainee,

We thought it best to send you a card instead of the traditional e-mail. The computer is a little too bright and noisy for someone in your present condition. We would just like to say that you are making excellent progress and when you feel up to it, you may like to consider the following:

We are what we think. All that we are arises with our thoughts. With our thoughts we make the world. Also, if you have faith as small as a mustard seed, you can say to a hill, 'go from here to there' and it will go. You can do anything.

With love from us all

xx

11

TEARS OF A CLOWN

Every day brought a new experience. I no longer needed to plan my days. Life had become like an unfolding tapestry, it was colorful with a rich texture unlike my previous way of life which was dull and flat. I practiced and practiced everything The Barefoot Indian showed me and applied everything I had heard. I didn't just sit back. I tested everything. I wouldn't accept anything as real until I experienced it for myself. My life was for learning, exploring and going beyond the boundaries. I had to be extreme in order to know the supreme.

This particular day I went to a circus which had come to town. It was a small family run circus so the crowds were not too big. The circus was very traditional as opposed to the larger, more modern ones. It was very well put together and very entertaining. When the first half was over I decided to remain seated in the interval while everyone else went outside for refreshments.

"Having fun?" asked The Barefoot Indian.

I looked around but I couldn't see her.

"Where are you?" I asked.

"Everywhere," she replied. "You don't have to see me in order to know I am with you."

"I assume there is something for me to learn from that?" I questioned.

"Of course," she replied.

Just as she said that she appeared in the seat next to me.

"Have the clowns been on yet?" she asked.

"No, not yet."

"Oh good, I like the clowns," she said.

"I am not going to ask why," I said.

We sat for a while in silence as I tried to learn the lesson that she had just given me when I suddenly remembered the day in the park when we were talking to each other without moving our mouths.

"Why can we talk to each other without moving our mouths?" I asked.

"Everyone talks without moving their mouths," she replied.

"What do you mean?"

"You are only ever communicating with your heart, but your belief in separation causes you to deny this. For example, when you greet someone, the greeting arises from within your heart first and then your mind puts that feeling in to words. When you no longer rely on the mind only the feeling remains."

"Let me ask you, when you have a conversation do the words come out first and then you know what to say or do you know what to say first and then the words come out?"

"I know what to say first and then the words come out," I replied.

"You believe you have to put what's in your heart into words because another cannot know what is in your heart. As we are all cut from the same cloth, what is in your heart is known. Words are not needed, all is known; nothing can be kept hidden. Telepathy is your natural state. You communicate soul to soul," she said "You can know everything about someone without them saying a word to you."

"I think I understand," I said.

I looked around at the audience who were beginning to return and it was true. If I listened to my own heart it told me everything about what was in their hearts.

The interval was over and the circus began. The clowns came out first and were very funny in a stupid kind of way. The Barefoot

Indian chuckled away. When they were finished I asked,

"Why do you like them so much?"

"Because they don't take themselves seriously," she replied.

"Oh, I thought you were going to say something profound," I said.

"I did," she said. "But I can be more profound if you would like?"

"Yes please."

"Well, let's take the clowns for example. Imagine if a clown came out and took on the role of the ring master. He takes the role seriously, standing there with authority but is dressed in a stupid outfit and has the most enormous feet. He proceeds to speak to the audience with a commanding voice but it just doesn't seem right, a clown taking on the role of a professional."

"The audience can see he is trying to be something that he is not. They begin to boo him and shout for him to get off. He is horrified as he desperately wants to be taken seriously but leaves the ring with his head bowed in shame. The clown is devastated, but all is not lost. The only thing the clown has failed to realize is that the audience were only pointing out to him that he wasn't being what he is, he wasn't doing what he was best at; he was trying to be something that he wasn't. The only reason they did not like him being a ring master is that they could see he was a clown."

"So it is with life, when you are persecuted and made fun of and fail to achieve what you set out to achieve. Take heart, for life is only pointing out to you that you are failing to be what you are not. Realize this, and it frees you to be what you are," she said.

"Yes, I can see that!" I said. "If you are a genius and are trying to act stupid, you are destined to fail."

"Absolutely," she said.

"But how do you be what you are? How do you know what you really are?" I asked.

"You can only be what you are by ceasing to be what you are not!" she replied.

She then continued "When you are no longer interested in

acting, pretending, or trying to be what you are not, what you truly are remains."

"But how do you know that you are pretending?" I asked.

"Like the clown trying to be the ring master, when you are trying to be other than what you are, it is painful, uncomfortable, unsatisfactory and miserable. You will always have the sense that something is missing and life will never seem quite right. That is how you will know."

Suddenly she said "I have to dash; I'll see you in a short while."

With that she was gone.

I wonder where she had to go in such a hurry I thought to myself.

I didn't have to wait long to find out. The next act was The Barefoot Indian! I was surprised to say the least. She entered the ring on the most magnificent horse. It was a white stallion, with the most amazing glossy, shiny coat and a long wavy mane and tail. She cantered around the ring and gave the most breathtaking display of bareback riding I had ever seen. It was as if both horse and rider were one. The horse's attention was totally absorbed with The Barefoot Indian and she was as absorbed with the horse.

What is she doing? How did she get out there? I thought as I watched her going around.

"I am enjoying myself and there is no one who can deny me," I heard her words through my heart as she looked up at me and winked.

After her display of horsemanship and a standing ovation, she came and sat next to me as the circus was coming to an end.

"That was incredible," I said.

"Thank you," she said. "Have you enjoyed the circus?"

"Very much," I said.

"There's just one more thing to learn from today" she said.

"What's that?" I asked.

"As you have seen today every performance was an act, performed to the highest standard. The audience responded accordingly, they thoroughly enjoyed what they saw, marvelled at the talent and their applause reflected their appreciation. It could equally have gone the other way, where the performance was poor and the audience were disappointed at paying for such a shoddy show. Their lack of applause would reflect this."

"The moral of this is: if you don't like the reaction you get, get your act together!"

"Will do!" I said.

"By the way," she said, "Head Office is so pleased with your progress that they feel you will soon be ready to take the exam."

"Really!" I exclaimed. "When?"

"Whenever you feel ready," she replied.

"I don't feel ready yet," I said.

"That's OK. I'm sure you will feel ready soon," she said.

Blimey! I thought, feeling very smug. I have managed to get this far with no healing involved. Brilliant! I suspect I can go all the way without doing any after all!

"I heard that," said The Barefoot Indian.

Nothing is hidden, I thought as we made our way out of the tent. Once we were outside I felt compelled to ask another question.

"Before you go, can I ask you something?"

"You can ask me anything," she replied.

"Who am I? I asked.

"Now that is a question," she said, "but only you can answer it."

I headed home, still in amazement at The Barefoot Indian's riding ability. I hope that I can do that one day, I thought.

I arrived home and before doing anything else I wrote in my notebook:

ME

My Nose – Perfect!

My Grief – Unnecessary

My Breath – Alive

My Motives – Deceitful

My Pockets – Empty

My Wealth – Endless
My Vision – Clear
My Mind – Redundant
My Heart – Open
My Hearing – Alert
My Mouth – Silent
My Judgments – Powerless
My Favorite Question – What do you mean?
My Opinions – Limiting
My Butt – Sore!
My Face –Beautiful
My Thinking – Wrong
My Ability – Amazing
My Feet – Can walk on water
My Room – Spinning!
My Laughter – Flows
My Talking – Quiet
My Acting – Not believable

I checked my e-mails and to my surprise there weren't any. How strange I thought, that's most unusual. I was just about to switch off my computer when, to my relief I received my usual e-mail from Head Office:

Internal Memorandum

Dear Trainee,

Did you think that we had forgotten you? Impossible! Here is your reminder for the day.

1. The only real failure in life is not to be true to the best one knows.

2. Three things which cannot be long hidden: the sun, the moon and the truth.

We love you.
B xx

12

TO BE OR NOT TO BE

I was in heaven! I was horseriding across an open field, the sun was dazzling and calmness filled the air. I cantered from one end of the field to the other; it was smooth and effortless, the horse and I were in perfect unison. Life was flowing from me and to me in a never ending cycle; it was without end. Anything I thought of was so; I was at one with everything. I jumped from my horse and sat among the wild flowers, their colors were vibrant. I looked around and noticed that the leaves on the trees were as green as emeralds and the sky was as blue as the ocean. Everything I looked at was alive! The peace I felt was beyond anything I could have imagined, there was no fear here, there was nothing to fear. I was without selfishness, judgments and opinions. Those motives and thoughts had passed away and in passing away, my true self was exposed. I was unlimited; to me all things were possible, there was nothing I did not know. I was dead but was now alive again! All was perfect.

After a short while, I stood up to get back on my horse. From a standing position I jumped and flung myself over the horse's back. I obviously used too much force and went right over its back and hit the ground on the other side. I landed with a thud and it was then that I suddenly realized that I had been dreaming.

I woke up with a jolt. I sat upright in bed and there sitting on the bedroom chair in front of me was The Barefoot Indian.

"Good morning," she said.

"Good morning," I replied.

I tried to gain my composure as quickly as possible and bring myself back to reality.

"I have just had a wonderful dream," I said, trying to sound wide awake.

"Yes, I know," she said.

"How do you know?" I asked.

"I know everything," she said "just like you did in the dream."

"So I don't need to tell you about it?"

"No," she replied.

As I began to regain consciousness I said, "If only life was really like that."

"But it is," she said with authority. "The trouble with you is that in your own little world you say that perfection is a dream and imperfection is a reality. In my world I say perfection is a reality and imperfection is a dream. Wake up!"

I flung myself backwards on the bed and stared at the ceiling, contemplating what she had just said. Then I asked,

"In my dream everything was perfect, I saw perfection. Why was that?"

"You saw perfection because you were being perfect," she said.

"So if I see imperfection is that because I am being imperfect?"

"Yes, you only ever see what comes from the heart of you. Your life only ever reflects what you hold to be true."

She continued, "I shall leave that with you to contemplate later if you wish as there is another reason I came here today."

"Oh," I said, "What's that?"

"Well, I wanted to catch you early today as I would like to give you another challenge," she continued, "that's if you are willing?"

"Yes, I am" I said, feeling excited. "What would you like me to do?"

"Continue your day as planned but there will be an opportunity that comes your way when you can decide whether to be or not to be."

"What do you mean, to be or not to be?" I questioned.

"In your world you have a choice. As we have previously

discussed you can either be what you are or you can deny what you are. It is rather like standing in a brilliantly lit room but you choose to close your eyes and say it's dark. You are like the brilliantly lit room, light, bright, shining, clear and all-powerful but you stand there with your eyes closed and insist that you are dark, dull, dim and powerless." She said, "Today you will have an opportunity to shine, to be all-powerful or you can be dull and powerless. It is up to you what you will be."

"But why would I do that?" I said. "Why would I deny myself like that, why would anyone? Surely, if that is true why would I deny the light, that which I am?"

"Fear," she replied. "You have got so used to walking around in the dark that you fear the light, the unknown. You are so used to it that you don't even recognize that it's dark. You also believe all the others in the room when they say it is dark, the more who say it, the more it must be true. Stand alone, stand up and be counted, open your eyes and see."

"I'll try" I said with uncertainty.

"Good luck," she said. "I will call in again later to see how you got on."

"OK. Bye for now," I said.

She then departed and left me on my own. I leapt out of bed to begin my day.

'Continue your day as planned,' The Barefoot Indian's words went through my mind.

I did just that. I washed and dried some clothes had a leisurely breakfast and then I got ready to go to the nearest city to do some early Christmas shopping. As I was leaving, in my mind I thought back over the morning just to double check that I had not missed the 'opportunity.' I felt confident that I had not missed it and carried on with my day.

The weather was a typical winter's day, wet, miserable and breezy. It was not the best day to do Christmas shopping but I was determined to get most of the things on my list. After a couple of hours of shopping, I went to a café for a hot chocolate and reflected on the day so far. Nope, I thought, I had not had the 'opportunity' yet. I left the café to continue shopping but by mid afternoon I had had enough so I headed home. The traffic was really heavy and my journey home took some time. I arrived home slightly disappointed that there had been no 'opportunity' and I carefully scrutinised my day so far just to make sure.

I had dinner and then set about doing the ironing. As I was merrily ironing and lost in my own thoughts, The Barefoot Indian suddenly walked into the room.

"Hello again," she said. "How did you get on?"

"Well there was no 'opportunity'" I said. "It was just a normal day."

"Even normal days are full of 'opportunities'," she said. "In any moment you have the choice to open your eyes, to see the light".

"Point taken," I said. "But I was waiting for a particular incident."

"You see you are so used to the dark that you couldn't even see the incident, to you it was normal," she said.

"What incident?"

"You tell me," she continued. "Go through your day again and see if you can see it the second time around."

This must have been my tenth time of going over my day without seeing anything but I didn't let on.

"OK," I said. "When you left I washed and dried some clothes and had a leisurely breakfast…" I proceeded to go through my day. I just got to the part when I had had my hot chocolate and left the café when The Barefoot Indian shouted

"Stop there." She continued, "What did you see when you came out of the café?"

"Erm… Nothing really, just lots of people shopping," I answered.

"When you came out of the café and turned right up the high street what was to the right of you?"

"A shop," I said.

"And what was outside of the shop?" she asked.

I really had to think hard about it and then all of a sudden it came back to me.

"Well, there was a homeless man, holding up a piece of cardboard which said 'feed me'."

"And what did you do?" she asked.

"I ignored him," I said. Embarrassed, I tried to justify my actions to her, "I didn't really pay him much attention; I was too busy trying to get to the next shop."

"Do you think it normal for another to be homeless and hungry?" she asked. "Is that why you paid him no attention? He was just an outcast from society and had nothing to do with you? Is that what you think?"

"I guess I do," I said hanging my head in shame, "but I can't really see what I could have done."

"How can you see what you could do for him when you don't even acknowledge him?" she said.

I was stuck for words.

"How did you feel when you passed him? What were your thoughts?"

"He made me feel uncomfortable, fearful I guess. He looked so miserable, dark and dull and I felt so powerless. It was easy for me to look the other way and ignore him."

"So there you had it, the 'opportunity'" she said, "in that moment you found it easier not to be, to keep your eyes closed and continue with the darkness. Not only did you keep yourself in darkness you made sure he remained there too."

Feeling incredibly guilty I turned to her and said, "What can I do?"

"All is not lost. If I give you another opportunity in this moment to be or not to be, which one will it be?" she asked.

"To be," I answered. "Definitely!"

No sooner had I said the words and in a movement quicker than that of blinking my eyes, I found myself standing outside a mud house somewhere in India. The air was dry and hot, dust seemed to fill the atmosphere.

Sitting outside the house was a young woman with a small, thin child in her arms. They were clearly very poor and the child was very hungry; it was crying into its mother's chest. I stood there in front of them and could see in her other hand she was holding an empty bowl. She had the biggest brown eyes and was staring straight into mine. She held out her bowl to me. With that and without thinking I held out my hands and rice just poured forth from my hands into her bowl; the rice came from nowhere, it just poured from within my hands. Although the rice was appearing from my hands the source of it was deep within my heart (that is the only way I can describe it). When her bowl was full she looked at me, her face was beaming and her eyes shone with relief. With tears in her eyes she said to me,

"Thank you. I knew you would come, I have been asking."

No sooner had she finished speaking than I was back in my room with The Barefoot Indian.

"Well done," she said. "What did it feel like to finally be?"

"That was awesome, beyond words, effortless. It was the most natural thing in the world."

"I shall now leave you in peace," she said. "You need to reflect on what you have just done."

"Thank you," I said.

"I didn't do anything; it was all down to you," she said.

She then left.

I sat quietly. I needed to take in what had just happened. I was not in India in my mind only; I was there with my body. The realization of what had just occurred hit me like lightening. Tears welled up from my heart like a fountain, tears of joy flowed down my face, I could not stop them. Surely, only the 'Unlimited' could do such a thing.

As I sat crying I wrote:

ME

My Nose – Perfect!
My Grief – Unnecessary
My Breath – Alive
My Motives – Deceitful
My Pockets – Empty

My Wealth – Endless
My Vision – Clear
My Mind – Redundant
My Heart – Open
My Hearing – Alert
My Mouth – Silent
My Judgments – Powerless
My Favorite Question – What do you mean?
My Opinions – Limiting
My Butt – Sore!
My Face – Beautiful
My Thinking – Wrong
My Ability – Amazing
My Feet – Can walk on water
My Room – Spinning!
My Laughter – Flowing
My Talking – Quiet
My Acting – Not believable
My Dreams – Are a reality
My Reality – Is a dream
My legs – Can take me anywhere
My hands – Can only give
My Tears – Cleansing

That night I was so immersed in the events of the day that I didn't bother to check my e-mails.

I awoke the next morning after the most peaceful night's sleep that I had ever experienced. I woke up in the same position that I went to sleep in; it was if I hadn't moved through the night. I also had no dreams.

I dressed and while making some breakfast I suddenly remembered that I hadn't checked my e-mails the night before. I rushed to the computer eager to see what comments Head Office made regarding my trip to India. I had one new message in my inbox. I opened it up and to my surprise it wasn't from Head Office, it was from my Mother; the biggest surprise was the fact that she had managed to send an e-mail. She had sent me a poem that made me chuckle out loud; how very true it was:

To my Dearest Daughter

Your earthly life, my Mother dear
For your information
Is solely now to seek the truth
And to stop reincarnation
This is what my Daughter said
When airing all her knowledge
'wow' I thought I know she's right
And she's never been to college
So on the path I started out
The 'Ultimate' to find
But, wait a bit, what is the truth?
Is it in my mind?
No! No! she cried that's not the way
The answer is in the heart
You only have to ask you know
Your spirit does its part
I've been into the head and into the heart
And down upon my knees
I've searched and looked and read some books
And done my best to please
Answers there have been a few
My spirit soared aloft
My brain is going round and round
I think it's going soft
Just when I think I've found the way
And thinking thoughts of heaven
Not yet! She says in voice so sweet
No knowledge has been given
So as I keep on keeping on
Amid this vast illusion
I also suffer Daughter dear

FROM TOTAL BLOODY CONFUSION!
Love Mum xxx

13

BLOCKBUSTER

It was some time later when I saw The Barefoot Indian again. I assumed this was to give me time to reflect on past events; to gather my thoughts and bring them up to date. This I did. I viewed it a little like revision.

It was on one particular afternoon when I was enjoying a lazy day that she popped in. It was a Sunday and not much was happening; it was the type of day which would be perfect to spend lounging on the sofa watching a good movie.

"Hello," she said. "How are you?"

"Great!" I replied.

"Of course you are," she said.

She went over to the sofa and sat down. I noticed that she was carrying a small padded envelope but decided not to question her about it; she would tell me what it was if and when.

"I'm so glad you have come, I have some questions for you," I said.

"Good. After all, that's what I am here for," she said, smiling. "Fire away!"

"Well," I began, "Why is it so difficult to accept the 'Unlimited' as a reality?"

"It isn't," she replied. "Accepting the 'Unlimited' as a reality is easy; the difficult bit is not seeing the limited as an unreality. You hold on so tightly to your limitations."

"I would agree with that," I said.

After briefly absorbing her words I continued with my next question.

"I feel as though I have been searching for something all my life but without really knowing what I am searching for. Is it the 'Unlimited'?"

"Let me put it this way. Your life is rather like using your computer," she said. "When you start to do a search on the World Wide Web, you type in what it is you are looking for and it leads you to a page. As you read the page another link catches your interest and so you click on it. This then takes you to another page which you read with interest, then another link catches your eye and so you click on that. Again it takes you to another page and so it goes on. This can go on for hours. Hours later you have forgotten what it was you were originally searching for; you have got lost in the web of trails. This is what your mind is like; one thought leads to another and another and so on. In fact without getting too technical, the web was actually designed as a direct result of the way in which you think."

"You are constantly searching for something, but you have got so lost you can't remember what it is."

"Yes, I can see that," I said.

She continued, "Take heart though, it is not the search that is important, it is the one who is searching that is of importance. At least you know that whilst you are searching there is always someone who is doing it, but eventually you tire of the searching and when you cease to search, what remains?"

"The one who was searching," I replied.

"Correct," she said. "The one who was doing the searching was in truth the very thing you were searching for."

"So I am not searching for the 'Unlimited,' I am searching for me?" I asked.

"What makes you think that they are different?" she laughed. "I shall leave that one with you."

"So be it!" I said.

"Yes, so be it!" she said.

I went to the kitchen to make some drinks although I wasn't quite sure why when The Barefoot Indian could easily make some appear, but I guess old habits die hard. By the time I had made the drinks and returned back to the living room, I had another question for her.

"When I made my little trip to India, I was actually physically there, but I do not understand how. How was that possible? I have been thinking about it since it happened. Can you help to shed some light on it for me please?"

"Yes," she replied. "If you observe your body it is only ever carrying out what you think."

"What do you mean?" I asked, intrigued.

"When you walked out to the kitchen a few minutes ago, you thought about going there and your body carried out that instruction. It only ever does what you want it to do. It does not have a mind of its own. In truth you and the body are one and the same."

She continued. "The body is whatever you say it is. It can only do whatever you think it can do. A common error is that you believe you are ruled by the body when in reality the body is ruled by you."

"So, what you are saying is that when I went to India it was, in principle, just like going out to the kitchen to get a drink," I said.

"Yes, but you found another way of getting there," she said. "You got there without any limitations. To move the body without any limitation is to know your destination and realize you have already arrived. Practice this, the results will surprise you."

"I will." I promised.

"But I don't have any control over the fact that the body ages or gets sick do I?" I said questioningly.

"Let me give you something else to think about," she said. "If that which makes all life possible is perfect, magnificent and awesome, beyond limitation, infinite, all loving, pure and alive, how could it possibly create something that ages and gets sick? Why would it do that?"

"Well, it wouldn't, it couldn't," I answered.

"I'll leave that one with you to contemplate," she said.

We sat for a while in silence. Suddenly The Barefoot Indian reached to the side of her for the small padded envelope.

"Oh, I nearly forgot," she said. "I have brought a DVD for us to watch. Would you like to see it?"

"What is it?" I asked.

"It's a movie."

"Yes, that would be nice," I said "What is it called?"

"The title is Healing Through the Eyes of a Master." she said.

"And what is it about?" I asked nervously.

"Healing through the eyes of a Master" she replied enthusiastically. "It was filmed some years ago and it depicts how a Master viewed the world and how he healed the sick."

"Sounds fascinating," I said sarcastically.

"I think you are now ready to watch it," she said.

"OK, if I must," I said.

I took the DVD from her with some degree of hesitation. The box was designed with a swirl of vivid yet peaceful colors and the title was written across the top. I placed the DVD in the machine and sat back to watch the movie.

I reluctantly pressed the remote control and the movie started. The opening shot was of vast, open countryside in a very hot country. The landscape was arid and dusty with a peppering of green trees in the distance. It looked rather barren and deserted. As the movie progressed it was quite extraordinary because as a viewer it was like I was looking through the eyes of somebody else. It had been shot using a technique I had never witnessed before; I was viewing it as though I was the main character.

Watching from this new perspective I looked around. The light was very bright and everything seemed to be alive. The trees were not like we normally see them; it was as if they were breathing. The sun in the sky and the hills in the distance were shimmering with a golden light; everything was covered in a halo of light. The sheep that were grazing next to me were not afraid of me, they had nothing to fear. Every color was vibrant and sharp and all things were crystal clear, as though everything was in sharp focus.

The movie continued to pan in and out of my surroundings and I was awestruck by the beauty and peace that was all around. Suddenly I could see a tall man walking up the hill toward me. He was wearing a scruffy brown robe but he too was surrounded by a haze of golden light which was not only all around him but also radiating from within him. As the man got nearer to me I started to see something peculiar. All I could see when I looked at this man was light, he was perfect in every way; he was alive and well. Yet, for some strange reason I could see that he thought he was sick, he was holding the side of his face as though he was in pain and he was crying. I could not see why. There was nothing wrong with him; it was as if he was dreaming. Then the Master or whoever's eyes it was I was looking through, raised their hand and gently placed it on the man's face. With that the man sighed with relief and began to smile.

"Thank you," he said as he fell to his knees.

All the supposed pain had gone. The man then stood up and went on his way.

I quickly pressed the pause button on the remote control to stop the DVD and turned to The Barefoot Indian.

"That man just thought he had been healed!" I exclaimed. "Yet there was nothing wrong with him."

"Yes I know, funny isn't it?" she said, smiling.

"But the Master went along with it. Why?" I asked.

"The man was dreaming, he thought he was sick, the Master simply woke him up; got him to see that there was nothing wrong," she said. "He so loved the man that he wanted him to open his eyes and see."

"But how did he get him to open his eyes?" I enquired.

"By touching him," she replied.

"When a child is asleep in bed and having a bad dream, how would you wake the child up?"

"I would gently touch the child," I replied.

"That's right," she said, "and that's exactly what the Master did."

"But why did the man not go to someone else, why did he go to the Master? I asked.

"Because the Master is awake," she replied. "Only those who are awake can wake-up those who are sleeping."

"That's awesome!" I said. "But it is so simple, there is nothing to heal. I have worried so much about healing and yet all I need to do is give a nudge!"

"Well, if you want to put it like that, yes," she said.

"But how did he know the Master was awake?" I asked enthusiastically.

"Like a moth he was attracted to the light. If you observe a moth on its way to the light it can appear to be a little crazy, frantically flying around banging into things as if it's blind. It may look like the moth is lost and cannot find its way but it knows exactly where it is going. When it eventually finds the light and rests there, all is well; the moth is at peace, calmness rules," she replied.

"I couldn't have put it better myself!" I said, for it truly was like watching a moth making its way to the light.

I eagerly switched the DVD back on. I wanted to see more. I watched as the man walked back down the hill, where he passed another man heading our way. This time the man was limping and again I could not see why. He looked perfect to me, yet to him, somewhere in his mind, his leg was bad. The Master put both hands around his leg and bingo the man was 'healed.'

I watched the rest of the movie with interest. There were plenty more examples but I do not want to bore you with all the details; it would be best if you see the movie for yourself.

It lasted for about two hours and when it was over I sat there, dumbfounded unable to move.

"Did you enjoy that?" asked The Barefoot Indian.

"Yes, very much," I replied.

"Did you learn anything from it?"

"I learnt an awful lot, yet in reality there was nothing to learn," I said, smiling.

I then continued, "If I had to sum up the truth, the 'Unlimited', in one sentence I would have to say it is 'what I have always known but never acknowledged'."

"It's funny that you should say that," she said.

"Why?" I questioned.

"Well, because a colleague of ours has written a book called, 'What I have always known but never acknowledged'. It's an excellent little book; it helps to unravel all the illusions which you hold to be true; like water dripping onto a boulder, it gently erodes the boulder away."

"Why did I not get a copy of it?" I asked.

"You have me," she said.

Then without thinking, the words just tumbled from my mouth, I said "I think I am now ready to sit the exam."

"Brilliant!" she exclaimed. "I shall set things in motion for you."

"OK," I said.

It was then time for her to go. I thanked her for bringing the movie over and she kindly said I could keep it.

"I will be in touch very soon," she said. "Bye for now."

And then she was gone.

What a brilliant way to spend a Sunday afternoon, I thought, watching a blockbuster like that.

Feeling on a high I grabbed my notebook and wrote:

ME

My Nose – Perfect!
My Grief – Unnecessary
My Breath – Alive
My Motives – Deceitful
My Pockets – Empty
My Wealth – Endless
My Vision – Clear
My Mind – Redundant
My Heart – Open
My Hearing – Alert
My Mouth – Silent
My Judgments – Powerless

My Favorite Question – What do you mean?
My Opinions – Limiting
My Butt – Sore!
My Face – Beautiful
My Thinking – Wrong
My Ability – Amazing
My Feet – Can walk on water
My Room – Spinning!
My Laughter – Flowing
My Talking – Quiet
My Acting – Not believable
My Dreams – Are a reality
My Reality – Is a dream
My legs – Can take me anywhere
My hands – Can only give
My Tears – Cleansing
My Body – Has no boundaries
My Health – All's well

I then switched on my computer and received the following message:

Internal Memorandum

Dear Trainee,

We are so pleased that you now feel ready to sit the exam. We will contact you shortly regarding that. However, in the meantime, if you could contemplate the following you may find it of some help.

1. Every human being is the author of his own health or disease.
2. You can search throughout the entire universe for someone who is more deserving of your love and affection than you are yourself and that person is not to be found anywhere. You yourself, as much as anybody in the entire universe, deserve your love and affection.
3. Just as a candle cannot burn without fire, men cannot live without a spiritual life.

We look forward to seeing you very soon.

With love from all of us,
Xx

14

THE FINAL COUNTDOWN

I had noticed from past experience that when Head Office or The Barefoot Indian said they would be in touch soon, this really didn't mean anything. I could be waiting months for them to get in touch with me. My view of soon means within a week or two but to them time hardly seemed to exist. This, I was beginning to understand. Time is a limitation; a device for the mind to keep everything in order, but to the 'Unlimited' time is unknown.

I was feeling very confident about taking the exam but as the date was still unknown to me, I pushed it to the back of my mind. I had arrived at the point where there was no more I could do. The training seemed to be over and all I could do was wait to hear from Head Office. I decided to make the most of this period by practising and going over everything that I had learnt.

I was still struggling slightly with moving the body without limitation. I could move the body without any problems but it was the destination that was causing me the headache. For example, I would arrive in the bathroom when it was the kitchen I was heading for, or I would end up in Liverpool when I was trying to get to London. I didn't think this was too much of a problem; I just needed to tweak things a little. At least I was moving. As someone once said, 'it is better to travel well than to arrive.'

Anyway, as they say 'practice makes perfect' and this was the case with me. I eventually mastered the art of moving without limitation. I could be wherever I wanted to be and be whatever I wanted to be in less than a blink of an eye. It was shortly after I had just perfected the art that The Barefoot Indian arrived.

"Well done!" she said with a big grin. "You are now ready to take the exam. We have been waiting for you to finalize things and now you have."

"I didn't realize you were waiting for me," I said.

"Yes, that's the way it works." She continued, "You determine everything. Nothing happens in your life without your say so."

"Yes, of course!" I said, laughing. "That one had slipped my mind, thanks for reminding me."

I was very excited to see her as she could have only come for one reason and that was to give me the details of when and where the exam would take place.

"Have you come with news about the exam?" I asked.

I waited with anticipation as she made her way across the room and gracefully sat down in the large comfy chair.

"Yes," she replied, "you will be taking it this afternoon."

"This afternoon?" I repeated, suddenly feeling nervous. "Where do I have to go?"

"Nowhere, the paper will be e-mailed to you. You can then fill it out and then send it back to Head Office," she said.

"Oh," I said. "How do they know I won't cheat?"

"How could you?" she said. "Only you know the answers."

"But you know the answers," I said.

"No, I don't," she stated. "Each person has their own answers. I only know my answers."

I got the feeling that no matter how much I had learnt or thought I knew there would always be something more to learn.

She continued, "However, I will sit with you throughout the exam just to observe things and be there should you need me, although I don't think you will."

"Thank you," I said. "That will be nice."

I was starting to feel more nervous, I was not quite sure why, perhaps I was starting to doubt my own ability.

"Don't worry too much about it, you will be fine; the written exam is not as important as the training assessment grades. The written exam is basically to tie up any loose ends, to make sure everything is in order. The paper will have been written with you in mind. It could be long or it could be short, we will not know until it arrives," she said.

"What time will they send the paper?" I asked.

"When it arrives" she replied.

There was nothing I could add to that.

She continued, "I thought we could spend this morning going over anything that you feel is still outstanding."

"That would be good," I said.

"Is there anything you would like to ask me, anything that you are still not certain of?" she asked in a tone as if she knew that there was something.

I thought for a while, scanning my brain for any little outstanding questions that were lurking around. I suddenly found one.

"Yes, there is," I said.

"Fire away then," she said.

"Well, when I was at Head Office for my interview, I remember JC saying that there was only one solution to any problem and that there is only one thing to ever know."

"Yes, that's right, carry on," she said.

"I fully understand that there is only one solution to any problem and that solution has to be the 'Unlimited.' I can see that all problems come from limitations and the one solution is to be unlimited but I don't understand the second part, that there is only one thing to ever know." I paused for a moment and then continued, "What is the one thing to ever know? I have thought about this throughout the training but I am still none the wiser. Could you help me with this?"

"Not really, it is not for me to tell you. However I can say that you will get a chance to know the answer when you go to Head Office."

"When will I be going to Head Office?" I questioned.

"When you have finished your paper, we will go later today," she replied. "There is one final part of the exam that will take place at Head Office. It's a practical task."

"That's sounds exciting," I said. "When will I get the results?"

"Perhaps tonight if things go well," she replied.

"So in theory, if I pass I could get promoted tonight?" I asked.

"Yes, you probably will be promoted tonight," she said strangely knowingly.

"I can't wait!" I exclaimed excitedly.

"Well you won't have to for much longer," she said. "Now, is there anything else outstanding?"

"Yes, there is just one more thing. It's not hugely important but I have always wondered how many people actually applied for this job?"

"Only you applied!" she replied as quick as a flash.

"Only me?" I said with surprise. "I thought thousands of people would have applied."

"No, just you," she said.

"Why? How far was the ad circulated? How many people got to see the ad?"

"Only you saw the ad and only you responded," she replied.

I then found myself asking a question that I thought I would not be asking again.

"What do you mean?"

"All people are different. Everyone has their own unique sign, their own unique wake-up call. The best way to get your attention was to place an ad that appealed to you; we positioned it in a place where only you would look. We get the attention of others with what suits them. There are as many ways as there are people."

"That's really fascinating," I said. "I bet you can have some fun coming up with signs to grab people's attention."

"Yes, it is always amusing," she said. "The three wise men and a manger was a good one."

"What was yours?" I asked.

"My sign was in no way glamorous," she replied with a sigh. "I was thrown from my horse and knocked unconscious, it was while I was unconscious and in another state of mind that Head Office made contact with me."

"What a shame, that isn't at all glamorous!" I said, "but at least the outcome was the same."

"Yes the outcome was the same." She continued, "so you see, you are not 'the chosen one', there is no such thing. All are chosen if they will but read the signs that are all around."

"How wonderful," I said.

The conversation came to an end so I got up to check my computer to see if I had received the paper but it was yet to come. I am not sure why I checked as my computer would tell me if I had any new massages, I guess I was just being impatient through excitement.

"Do you feel hungry?" asked The Barefoot Indian.

"Not really, I don't think I could eat anything," I replied.

"Try to eat a little" she said, "It is going to be a long day. If you go to the kitchen you will find a little something there."

I took her at her word and went to the kitchen; sure enough there was a platter of smoked salmon sandwiches and some fruit juice. I carried them back in to the living room where we sat and ate lunch. As we were finishing I heard those familiar techno words coming from my computer: 'you have new mail' it said.

I leapt up and rushed over to the computer. I opened the e-mail and sure enough it was from Head Office.

"It's arrived!" I shouted excitedly.

"Great" she said. "Take your time, there is no need to rush. Finish your drink first and then you can begin."

I went and sat back down to finish my drink. I was feeling really nervous now so it was good just to sit for a while and to compose myself. Once I had calmed down a little I made my way over to the computer and read the e-mail.

Internal Memorandum

Dear Trainee,

We are delighted that you have come so far and we wish you all the very best with your exam. Observing your progress so far we feel very confident that you will sail through it.

As you are aware we have been assessing and marking you throughout your training period. Here are the marks for your practical exam:

Total score 90%

We felt it necessary to deduct 10% due to the resistance you experienced regarding the healing aspect. The resistance was unnecessary as you later found out but this made things slightly difficult for you. However, the pass rate on the practical exam is 70% so you are well above the pass mark. You have been awarded a Grade A. Congratulations!

If you would like to open the above attachment you will find the written exam paper. Please take your time, there is no rush, and feel free to use as many words as you require. Once completed please send the attachment back to us. We will then mark the paper and we will give you the results ASAP.

Good luck should you need it and we look forward to seeing you later today.

Until then,
All our love,
JC, B & K xx
P.S. A little reminder for you – He is able who thinks he is able!

When I had finished reading the e-mail I turned to The Barefoot Indian who was now standing next to me and said excitedly,

"I have passed the practical exam, I got 90%!"

"Well done," she said, sharing my excitement. "I knew you would do it."

I then eagerly opened the attachment. I noticed the heading written at the top of the page which read 'Exam paper for Messiah/Messiahress Level 1.'

"What does Level 1 mean?" I enquired of The Barefoot Indian.

"Don't concern yourself with that at the moment, I shall explain that to you later when you have finished the paper," she said.

"OK," I said. "You know best."

She then pulled up a chair next to me so she could see the screen.

"Are you ready?" she asked.

"Yep, let's do it," I replied.

I quickly scanned the paper just to see what was involved. The beginning of it, in parts, was very familiar. It was like the original application form that I had filled in previously.

"Why are some of the questions the same as the application form?" I asked her.

"To see if the answers have changed and if so, how they have changed. They mark you not only on the answers themselves but on how much your answers have altered."

"Oh, I see," I said. "Well I'd better press on with it".

Exam Paper for Messiahress
Level 1

Please answer all questions with total honesty!

PART 1

Achievements to date: *Passing the practical exam at Grade A*

Do you think life could be better: *No, it is perfect*

Do you know the meaning of life? *There isn't one. Life is forever unfolding*

Do you believe in God? *I believe in everything. All is*

As a whole, what is your view of mankind: *Dreaming*

If someone came to you for help, what would you do? *Wake them up*

If you could do anything in the world, what would it be? *Wrap my arms around it; embrace it*

Do you judge people? *No. There is nothing to judge*

Do you know who & what makes all life possible? *Yes, the 'Unlimited'*

Are you serene, calm & still? *Always*

Can you heal the sick? *In truth there is no sickness*

Can you walk on water? *Only a short distance, approximately three steps to date*

If 5,000 people needed feeding what would you do? *I would feed them*

Do you love your neighbor? *How could I not*

Please say why you would like the job of Messiahress....

I would have to say that I do not believe there is such a job as Messiahress. I would never call myself a Messiahress. A Messiah or Messiahress is what others would call you when they don't understand. When the 'Unlimited' is fully understood there is no such thing as a Saviour, there is only what is.

PART 2

In your own words please write a short analogy that would best describe human life.

Life is like a tree. Your thoughts and emotions are like the leaves and the tree is known by the leaves it displays. It doesn't matter how many leaves are on the tree or how tightly the leaves cling to the branches, for the tree will shed them all. When the last leaf has fallen away, the tree remains standing, revealed, bare and unhidden.

PART 3

Please list ten points that you would give to guide another

- *When you don't know what to do – do nothing*
- *If faced with a choice – do neither or both*
- *Always have courage*
- *Your instinct knows better than anyone*
- *Have integrity*
- *Peace comes from within. Do not seek it without*
- *Do not be concerned with how others treat you. Be concerned with how you treat others*
- *Expect the unexpected*
- *Be like the wind – have no thought of where you are going or where you have come from*
- *Whatever you think will be so*

PART 4

Please answer the following:

1. If you dissected the smallest grain of sand what would you find? *Life*
2. If you hold a flower in your hand what are you holding? *Perfection*

3. If you look at the moon what do you see? *Innocence*
4. If you place your hand in the ocean what do you feel? *Purity*
5. If you see a bird in flight what are you witnessing? *Freedom*
6. If you hear children playing what do you hear? *Laughter*
7. If you drink from a stream what does it taste like? *Nectar*
8. If you smell a rose what do you smell? *Tranquillity*
9. If you watch the sunset what do you see? *Stillness*
10. If you listen to the wind what do you hear? *Peace*

Please state what the above answers have in common
The 'Unlimited', that which is in all things and is all things.

PART 5
In your own words please come up with a meditation

My meditation for stillness

Sit quietly and close your eyes. Visualize yourself lying on your back and looking up at the sky. The sky is full of clouds which move quickly in front of the sun. Each cloud represents a thought or emotion. Allow the clouds to pass away, as each moment passes the clouds will become less and less. As the clouds become less frequent your attention will move to the sun. Every time a cloud appears just let it pass, don't do anything with it, it will go by. Keep your eyes on the sun and experience its light, its stillness. Allow the sun to speak to you. Do not give thought to what it might say, just allow yourself to hear it. Hear the light without expectation.

PART 6
This section is the final practical task and will be carried out at Head Office, please wait for further instruction.

Thank you, that completes this paper

Please e-mail this paper back to JC@I-am.org.uk

We will get the results back to you ASAP

So that was it, the exam paper. I sat back with relief that I had managed to complete it. I turned to The Barefoot Indian.

"Well that wasn't too bad. It was a lot shorter than I had imagined."

"It could have been longer as I previously mentioned. My exam had fifteen parts!" she said. "Are you ready to send it in?"

"Yes, I think I have covered everything," I replied.

I confidently pressed the send button and watched it disappear into the ether.

"How do you think I did?" I asked.

"I think you did very well," she replied.

"Do you think I will pass?"

"I think failure is impossible!" she replied knowingly.

I switched off the computer while asking, "What shall we do now?"

"We shall just sit back for a little while to give them a chance to mark your paper and then we can make our move to Head Office," she replied.

"OK," I said. "I shall chill out for a while."

We made our way back over to the sofa and chair and slumped down in them. I must have nodded off because the next thing I remember was The Barefoot Indian gently shouting, "Wake-up, we will be leaving shortly to go to Head Office."

I jumped up and quickly came around.

"Should I take anything with me, is there anything I need for the final task?" I asked.

"No, just yourself!" she then continued, "But you could take your notebook with you."

"My notebook?" I enquired, "Why?"

"Because it is not complete as yet" she replied. "You may like to finish it tonight."

I didn't question what she meant, she always seemed to know what she was talking about, so I grabbed my notebook and a pen and then we were off.

We arrived at Head Office. It was strange to be back. It seemed such a long time ago since I first nervously walked into the plush office. We walked through the door. The dazzling light and the subtle smell of jasmine which filled the air brought back memories of the interview and I proudly thought how far I had come since then. Everything was how I remembered it except one thing; it was completely empty. There was not a soul in sight. How strange, I thought, as we made our way toward the huge table at the far end, perhaps everyone has gone home; after all we had arrived in the evening.

"Where is everyone?" I asked.

"I am sure they will be here soon," she said. "Just take a seat and wait."

And so we did, we waited and waited but still no one appeared. All was quiet. After what seemed like ages I broke the silence.

"I thought I would get my results tonight," I said.

"Be patient," was her reply. "Just wait. The time will come."

"What are we waiting for?"

"We are waiting for you to do the final task," she said.

"But I don't know what it is yet."

"You will do," she said knowingly again.

"Can't you tell me?"

"No, you don't need me to tell you what it is, you already know what it is but you haven't realized it yet." She continued, "Just sit quietly and wait."

And so I did, I waited and waited, but still nothing came, nothing happened and I couldn't see that anything was going to happen. I stood up.

"I shall have to go to the loo," I said. "Is that all right?"

"Of course it's all right," she replied.

I made my way to the cloakroom and went to the loo. My mind was totally preoccupied. I couldn't work out what was happening or what I was meant to do. My head was whirling with thoughts. When I had finished I went over to the sink, I needed to splash some water on my face to refresh myself and to try and get some clarity. I bent down to bring the water up to my face; the water was cold but refreshing. I fumbled around for a towel and rubbed my face and that is when it happened; that was the moment.

As I was finishing drying my face and when I started to open my eyes, it became apparent that I was standing in front of a mirror. It was the first time I had looked in a mirror since the beginning of my training. I looked at myself and couldn't believe what I was seeing. Beauty radiated from me, a halo of golden light flooded the room; it was flowing from within me and was all around me. I was shimmering, I was alive and vibrant. My eyes were as clear as the morning dew and they had a depth to them that went on forever. My skin was flawless and my smile was as bright as the sun. In a single movement my mind, my body and my soul were one. All operated as one unit; separation was no more. I was complete. I was staring divinity in the face. I was all and all was me. I could try to write what I saw for an eternity but I still wouldn't be able to describe or put into words what I saw.

I stood there in awe of what I was seeing as the full realization was starting to sink in. I was the 'Unlimited.' Of course! I thought, I am the 'Unlimited' how could I not be; that which is all life, is me also. I am what I am! How could I not have seen that? I must have been blind. I heard the door to the cloakroom open and The Barefoot Indian approached me.

"It's me isn't it?" I said.

"What's you?" she enquired.

"I am the one thing, the only thing to ever know!"

"Yes," she said sweetly. "It is you."

"This was the final task!" I exclaimed. "I have searched for this all my life. I have been looking at it all the time; the 'Unlimited' God, Isness, Love, Light, the Source, whatever I have called it, whatever label I have given it, I have never until this moment called it myself.".

I turned to face her. She held out her arms and wrapped them around me. Tears of joy were welling up in her eyes.

"Welcome home," she whispered.

We embraced for a while. Nothing was said but in the embrace I could hear everything.

"Come," she said, "the others are waiting. They have arrived for you to do the passing out parade."

"What is the passing out parade?" I enquired.

"It is a tradition that when you qualify you have to walk through the room to the Head Office anthem," she said.

"What is the Head Office anthem?" I asked.

"It is a song that we have adopted as our own. It is our Hymn. The words express how you feel about yourself when you have completed the final task. It is sung in celebration of the 'I'," she said.

We made our way back to the room. As she opened the door I was pleasantly surprised to see the room was full with all the familiar faces. The room was bursting with life.

"Congratulations!" JC said as he approached me. "You have passed!"

"How could I not?" I said, laughing.

"Absolutely true!" he said. "Failure, as you now know, is impossible."

"But just to complete things, to round things up, I would just like to say that you have been awarded an A+ in your written exam. Well done! The promotion is all yours."

He then turned to address the room.

"Let the parade begin!"

The music started up and I immediately recognized the tune.

"I recognize that tune; that's the Barry White song; *You're the first, My last, My everything* I said to The Barefoot Indian.

"Yes it is," she said. "But we have adapted it ever so slightly for our own purpose."

Everyone in the room parted, making an aisle for me to walk up. As I began the walk the choir began to sing in celebration and everyone joined in...

I made my way up the aisle to the beat of the music. The whole room was singing to me. The words could not have been more appropriate and I could see why this was the song chosen to be the Head Office anthem.

When the instrumental section was playing everyone in the room was dancing and swaying their hands in the air. It was the most extraordinary sight to see. They then continued to sing to me with an emotion that I can only describe as being all loving and compassionate. Every word that they sang was sung with such sincerity.

When the anthem was over the party began. It was a wonderful celebration. If you ever get the chance to go to a party that is organized by all the spiritual leaders, prophets, gurus, sages, or enlightened beings, it is well worth it, especially to see them dance to the anthem! We partied through the night. The moonlight was shining into the room like a torch; I was certain that its slivery light was dancing also.

As the sun began to rise the party came to an end. It was then that I suddenly remembered something. I sought out The Barefoot Indian.

"You forgot to tell me what Level 1 meant on the exam paper," I said.

"Ah yes," she continued, "Level 1 is learning all the basics of who and what you are; the foundation if you like. When you have completed this you move on to Level 2."

"And what is Level 2?"

"Level 2 is putting into practice, demonstrating, living and perfecting everything you have learnt in Level 1," she said.

"And how do you do that?" I enquired.

"Anyway you choose but most people tend to go out there," she said pointing out of the window to the world, "it's the perfect classroom for demonstrating and perfecting everything you know."

"And how many levels are there?"

"There are infinite levels," she smiled. "But Level 1 is the most difficult and painful to achieve."

"What level are you on?" I enquired.

"Well, tonight I have just passed Level 2" she replied. "Thank you for allowing me to demonstrate what I know."

We looked at each other and smiled.

I sat around the large table and thought about what she had said and was already thinking about how I would go about completing Level 2. My thoughts were interrupted by The Barefoot Indian.

"There's just one more thing for you to do," she said.

"What's that?" I enquired.

"Complete your list," she said, as she handed me my notebook and pen.

I took it from her and wrote:

ME

My Nose – Perfect!

My Grief – Unnecessary

My Breath – Alive

My Motives – Deceitful

My Pockets – Empty

My Wealth – Endless

My Vision – Clear

My Mind – Redundant

My Heart – Open

My Hearing – Alert

My Mouth – Silent

My Judgments – Powerless

My Favorite Question – What do you mean?

My Opinions – Limiting

My Butt – Sore!

My Face – Beautiful

My Thinking – Wrong

My Ability – Amazing

My Feet – Can walk on water

My Room – Spinning!

My Laughter – Flowing

My Talking – Quiet

My Acting – Not believable

My Dreams – Are a reality

My Reality – Is a dream

My legs – Can take me anywhere

My hands – Can only give
My Tears – Cleansing
My Body –Has no boundaries
My Health – All's well
My Eyes – All seeing
My Identity – Mistaken
My Life – Divine
My Soul – Is light
My Spirit – Is free
My Self – I am
My list – Complete!

When I had finished writing JC came over.

"I know it's a little early yet but have you had any thoughts of what you will do next or where you will go to begin Level 2?" he asked.

"Yes I have," I answered. "I think I will hang around here for a while."

"How lovely, for all of us," he said. "May I ask why you have decided this?"

I took his hand and led him to the window.

"I suspect that if I stay here for a while and observe the world below, there will be someone out there who will glance up, they will feel compelled to look to the top of this tower towards the 'Unlimited' suite. They may not know why they are looking but when they do; I will go down there and fetch them, guide them here and bring them home."

"So be it," said JC.

"So be it," I said.

JC moved away from me and left me standing at the window alone. I continued to watch the sun rising, there was not a cloud in the sky. Not only could I see the sun rising in all its splendor but I experienced it with every fiber of my being. It was then that I fully understood the true meaning of the phrase 'the peace that passeth all understanding.'

The end
But- in truth, it is just the beginning.

For further information about the author please visit
www.thebarefootindian.co.uk

O

is a symbol of the world,
of oneness and unity. O Books
explores the many paths of whole-
ness and spiritual understanding which
different traditions have developed down
the ages. It aims to bring this knowledge in
accessible form, to a general readership, providing practical spirituality to today's seekers.

For the full list of over 200 titles covering:
ACADEMIC/THEOLOGY • ANGELS • ASTROLOGY/
NUMEROLOGY • BIOGRAPHY/AUTOBIOGRAPHY
• BUDDHISM/ENLIGHTENMENT • BUSINESS/LEADERSHIP/
WISDOM • CELTIC/DRUID/PAGAN • CHANNELLING
• CHRISTIANITY; EARLY • CHRISTIANITY; TRADITIONAL
• CHRISTIANITY; PROGRESSIVE • CHRISTIANITY;
DEVOTIONAL • CHILDREN'S SPIRITUALITY • CHILDREN'S
BIBLE STORIES • CHILDREN'S BOARD/NOVELTY • CREATIVE
SPIRITUALITY • CURRENT AFFAIRS/RELIGIOUS • ECONOMY/
POLITICS/SUSTAINABILITY • ENVIRONMENT/EARTH
• FICTION • GODDESS/FEMININE • HEALTH/FITNESS
• HEALING/REIKI • HINDUISM/ADVAITA/VEDANTA
• HISTORY/ARCHAEOLOGY • HOLISTIC SPIRITUALITY
• INTERFAITH/ECUMENICAL • ISLAM/SUFISM
• JUDAISM/CHRISTIANITY • MEDITATION/PRAYER
• MYSTERY/PARANORMAL • MYSTICISM • MYTHS
• POETRY • RELATIONSHIPS/LOVE • RELIGION/
PHILOSOPHY • SCHOOL TITLES • SCIENCE/
RELIGION • SELF-HELP/PSYCHOLOGY
• SPIRITUAL SEARCH • WORLD
RELIGIONS/SCRIPTURES • YOGA

**Please visit our website,
www.O-books.net**